MILLIONAIRE MENTORSHIP™

HOW TO BUILD A REAL ESTATE EMPIRE STARTING FROM SCRATCH

BY

TROY J. KEARNS

Editor - Robert Kearns

Publisher - TK Education LLC

ISBN: 978-0-578-39096-3

INTRODUCTION

IF NOT NOW, THEN WHEN?

I understand how scary it can be to learn something new, but every day that you procrastinate puts you a day further away from your goals. Tomorrow is not guaranteed, so why not live your best life, starting today?!

Most of us were taught the wrong basics in school for building wealth - you know the ones: Get a job, save, invest in stocks and mutual funds for your retirement. I don't remember being taught anything about money, except for what it looked like and what I could spend. There is a reason schools are set up to groom you to get a job. Our society functions on free-market principles and businesses need an ever-increasing labor force to fulfill the supply and accompanying service demands of the marketplace. I really get that and respect everyone who loves going to work and doing their jobs to keep our markets humming. However, if you have a desire to step away from the daily grind and grow your personal wealth, real estate is set up for you to succeed beyond measure, no matter your age, sex, religion, race, or disability. The level of reward for your work investing in real estate is all up to you, even if you have just a modest goal of living an easy, chill life without worrying about having enough to retire.

For most people, their largest investment is their home. The equity in their home is often referred to as their education and/or retirement fund. They should take the logic just a little further and try to own a few more houses as rentals for relatively easy passive income. All houses that are cared for gain in equity. Why not flip and make more money on one flip than your day job provides in two or three years and use that as an income supplement to feed a special fund? [If you have young kids, those college years will come before you know it, and guess what, tuition never grows smaller.] A wise man once told me, "You work a job for a paycheck and experience." If you are not learning or growing in your job, and you are looking for a change, get the DealMachine app on your mobile device (https://dealmachine.app.link/troy); and try Driving for Dollars to make some wholesale deals - you can't get hurt! Or, if you love your job, stay with it and do some real estate investing as a side hustle for now, to protect yourself from downturns. The ONLY thing that real estate discriminates against is attitude.

The very best attitude is one of possibilities and solutions, even as you encounter tough challenges. Understand that failure is part of learning. Failure teaches you more than success does. When you fell off your bike or stubbed your toe, that was a failure telling you to be careful. With all our available online programming, we have many ways for you to keep failure to a minimum. Both the Troy Kearns Channel on YouTube and www.troykearnschannel.com website encourage feedback and questions from our regular visitors and subscribers. I've already made lots of mistakes that I frequently talk about, so you can learn (painlessly and quickly) from them. Also, I am designing classes right now so that by the time this book is published, you will be able to register for your favorites. I plan to engage in direct coaching and set up some MasterMind meetups, where you can connect with others who are learning the principles and best practices of real estate investing. One of the surest ways to learn is from smart and smarter-than-you people, and a MasterMind meetup draws together a great group.

Everyone is good at something. I have learned how to be good at investing in real estate, but I did just about everything the wrong way when I first started. I still am succeeding because I never quit, focused on solutions, and learned from my errors. I did not have a full-time mentor, but you will have me full time with the 'magic' of the Troy Kearns Channel on YouTube, my website www.troykearnschannel.com, as well as social media presence on TikTok, Instagram, and Facebook. If you forget the exact web addresses, just Google my name, Troy Kearns. [Late-breaking update: Based on the advice of my new social media guru, we are dropping the word "Channel" from YouTube and social media as part of a rebranding effort. For the time being, you should be able to find me with or without "Channel" in searches.] We post inspirational content every day so you can 'learn to earn' on your schedule. Are you ready to jump in and start learning how you can get into real estate investing today and become financially successful?

START READING THIS BOOK AND GET YOUR ENGINE RUNNING!

REMEMBER

"It's not what you say out of your mouth that determines your life, it's what you whisper to yourself that has the most power!"

- Robert Kiyosaki

FOREWORD

I WROTE THIS book to help you learn basic, easy-to-use steps that I took, which have allowed me to retire at a very young age. However, I still work every day because I love what I do, and I'm having fun doing it. If I did not love the work involved in real estate investing, I would not do it. Housing is a fundamental human need, which will never go out of style; it provides a relatively easy approach to investing because it is understandable to all of us. As I started out, my circumstances were bad, then became good, got bad, got worse, got better, and finally turned great, which they remain to this day. It was a long list of choices and decisions I made that transported me here. Your journey will be different because your goals and whole life are uniquely different from mine. Real estate will be the common denominator.

Most mistakes made in real estate, including some of the worst investments, are usually covered over time. Bad or questionable decisions about other things (over-extended credit, alcohol, drugs, infidelity) are what can destroy your world, so you need to make sure you manage and control 'other things' in your life along the road to success. As I get ready to publish this narrative of my journey and look back, I think about what I would like you to take from this book. I want you to gain inspiration and take action, but also to acquire a body of knowledge from the thousands of transactions of which I have been a part, and the hundreds of houses that I own or have purchased, renovated, and flipped. While you grow as an investor, you will have something to teach to someone else, as my mentors have taught me. Again, each person's journey is different from another's. The only thing you need to make certain of is that you DON'T QUIT. Real estate investing is not hard, but as with everything in life, you will make mistakes, and those mistakes are based on decisions made with the information available at the time. *Quitting is always an option, but solving the problem is what makes the money*. The primary reason I have been successful is simply that I look for long-term solutions to problems that I encounter every day, always with a focus on the solution first, the problem last. The bottom line is that this book can't do the work for you; you have to do it. Anyone who has a burning desire to succeed can do this: There are no specific skills or college degrees required. You just need a good attitude, a willingness to learn, and an ability to adapt to change. Your journey will not be the same as mine, and it won't be the same as another investor's, so do not compare yourself to others. Determine what is important to you and your family, including all your goals and desires, and then make your plan. As you hit goals, the needle will move, and you'll want more.

This book is filled with the right steps. They are based on me taking wrong steps at first, then correcting and going in the right direction. I know a lot of influencers preach, "Take on debt, take on leverage, don't be scared of this, that and the other thing," but what they fail to mention are the bad times. My first investment house was a condominium in Renton, Washington, which I bought for $112,000 in 2002. I turned that into a rental, where I was losing about $100-300 per month. That was not a smart move, but I didn't know any better. I figured, who cares about a small monthly loss if it's going up in value. In 2005, I sold it and made $12,000, which basically just covered my losses. [About that time, I started to care about 'small' losses.] During the foreclosure crisis in 2010, those condos were selling for $5,000-25,000. The listing prices stayed low for a couple of major reasons: The condo association did a special assessment for an upgrade that killed the selling prices, and all the condos for sale there had to be purchased for cash. When there are many foreclosures in condos, banks will not allow loans for development because of the risk that they see, so values plummet. Well, as I sit here today, those same condos are selling for $280,000-$320,000. My point is that had I hung onto that investment and plotted the value on a graph over time, there would be a large dip near the beginning and then a steep recovery line. The passage of time is on your side with investment in real estate. Cash flow may go up or down, but it's not a concern as long as you stay profitable every month. Market timing will only matter when it's time to sell.

As you become a more experienced real estate investor, you will realize that money is made on buying a property at a discount today and selling it for a profit tomorrow. Patience and time are your friends. If you end up having a property that will not sell as a flip, you should have plan B to rent it because sometimes that works better for you in the long run. Let me give you a fairly recent example. In 2016, I bought a property that was going into foreclosure; I literally took possession seven days before the bank did. The person who sold it to me had not made a payment since they bought the house, so almost $58,0000 in back payments was owed. In order to finalize the deal, I had to buy the property subject to reinstating the existing mortgage (more about that in a later chapter). I had given the seller some money up front and held some back until they moved out. When I was negotiating with the seller (the property was owned solely by the husband), staff checked the title to make sure it could be sold individually. Long story short, I got caught up in the couple's divorce, and the wife sued me. The attorney she hired didn't care about anything I had to say, and the fight cost me tens of thousands in attorney's fees. Nevertheless, I had plan B and was able to rent out the property. Thankfully, the wife ended the lawsuit, and the value of the property went up almost $60,000 from the two years it took me to clear the problem. I like to turn my money often (meaning, not have it stuck long in the property), so that was not an ideal situation, but it worked out because I made way more than I thought possible. I also learned a huge lesson: Never forget to buy title insurance on properties that you are flipping. [However, if cash is paid for a property, I don't believe title insurance is absolutely necessary - unless you intend to sell the property in the future because most property buyers expect title insurance (more on that later).]

I bought the house above, 'subject to,' so I was able to close with the owner signing over the deed/title and then having the mortgage reinstated in my name. Because I used that method, I felt it unnecessary to buy title insurance. Bad idea. The wife's attorney hit us with an action because he was looking to take a bite out of the insurance with a claim based on the wife not being on the title. The claim didn't hold water, and I did end up winning the case, but it was costly in money and time (aka money when you're investing). The moral of the story? Always get title insurance on your flips.

If the example above had been a rental with a clouded title (more on clouded titles later), I would not care because I look at rentals as "parking places" for my money. Flipping is all about turning your money, and in my experience, the best way you can make a lot of money is in real estate. In fact, smart and well-considered flipping is the not-so-secret secret to most of my success. Once you learn to get

the rhythm down by turning your money fast, it is possible to flip the same money three-to-six times per year. Each time you flip, your capital grows, and before long, you've acquired real wealth. In fact, if you do things right and stay in the game, you could earn enough to retire in five years. How's that for a goal? OK, so get on over to Chapter One: Invest in Yourself First - Set Goals.

YOU can do this!

My Dad shot this picture of me in the cockpit of a fighter jet in the hangar bay of the museum aircraft carrier Yorktown (CV-10) at Patriots Point, South Carolina in 2004. I think this was the first time I started thinking about owning my own jet. Are you ready for takeoff?

TABLE OF CONTENTS

DEDICATION

THIS BOOK WOULD not have happened without the encouragement of my loving and infinitely patient wife, Eden. I never really thought of myself as a writer until she helped me see that I could be one. Personally, doing something takes a higher priority over writing about it, so when sitting at a desk writing or dictating, I'm always thinking about what I should be doing instead. Fortunately, Eden took the time to gently convince me that I had a lot of knowledge in my field, as well as true-life experiences and stories that many people would appreciate reading about and find helpful. They say behind every man is a greater woman (sic), and this is certainly the case in my life. My wife is a force of nature. Her organizational skills, strong work ethic and devoted, caring nature have enabled our success as a couple, family and business enterprise. I'm very grateful for her persistence in nudging me to write this book and for all of the years that I've been able to turn to her and be supported in my endeavors.

Nearly all would agree that having children changes your life for the best. Most certainly, our twins, Conrad and Scarlett, have been wonderfully unexpected blessings in our lives, and give me daily motivation to build a legacy that will last long after I'm gone. I want Conrad and Scarlett to know that anything is possible, if you stay determined in your quest, no matter what it might be.

My Mom (Marsha), Dad (Bob), and sisters, Chelsea and Tara, have always been supportive of my family and me. I am very thankful for their caring spirits, as well as their can-do attitudes when called upon for help. We share strong bonds, and our common love of humor and laughter has helped us navigate safely through some emotionally turbulent waters. Special mentions go to my Grandfather Wendell, who taught me the value of hard work, and my Aunt Kathy, who introduced me to investing with a gift of stock. Also, I am very lucky to have good in-laws, cousins, friends, mentors, employees, and associates who have helped me during the good and not-so-good years.

It's impossible to name everyone who assisted me on my path, but I do want to recognize all above who have contributed to my success. This book is dedicated to you.

****

It's important to have a good support system of positive people around you because they help maintain the engine of your motivation. Also, keep the self-talk inside your head positive - belief in yourself is vital to success. It's easy for critics to drag you down, but your actions will show your true self, so ignore the chatter. Make sure you show your appreciation to everyone for daily acts of kindness, and don't forget to thank the people that help you to get where you are headed. If you don't have a strong support system now, then you'll need to acquire one. Mentors, like teachers, are emotionally invested in your success as foundational supporters, so try to start out with a real estate pro in your community and then add other mentors as you go.

CHAPTER
ONE

Invest in Yourself First - Set Goals

THERE IS ONE standout thing in every successful person I respect and admire: They teach goal-setting. That is why "Set Goals" is part of the title of the first chapter of my first book. You need to remember what's important to you and why you are working so hard. Constantly reviewing goals keeps you centered and focused on what you are doing now and the next thing coming.

I have adapted personal goal-setting over the last 20 years, sometimes being really good at it and sometimes needing to adjust. You will become a student of the process as you write down your daily, weekly, monthly, yearly, and three, five, and ten-year plans. When I first started, I just wanted to have ten homes that produced $5,000 per month. It was thrilling to achieve that mark, but then I asked myself, "Now what?" Once you reach your first big goal, the goal line is going to change, and you will adapt it to fit. The main thing is to keep a challenge in front of yourself, so you're operating at top performance, but make sure the challenge is one you can overcome. That's the key: Adapt and overcome. Don't set a goal so high that you can't reach it, but make it a challenge to keep your mindset as a winner in the game.

I have some rather crazy goals that I am going to share with you right now, just so you know that it's OK to think really big. Keep in mind that I have been setting and making goals to attain financial success for a long time. Now that I have reached a fairly high level of success, I want to: own a professional football or basketball team, acquire a jet, build large skyscrapers. There are apps that I have dreamed of developing, and I plan to put one together with the help of a great app developer (partnerships get big things done - think Lewis and Clark expedition; Bill Gates and Paul Allen, founders of Microsoft). Dream big, aim high and surround yourself with people who encourage you.

Don't be afraid to dream big! Here I am peering up at a large parking garage that I want to buy in the Midwest. I started with nothing but a burning desire.

Who are you hanging around with? If you are hanging around with individuals whose priorities are not in line with yours, you may want to ask yourself why. You will do well if you share your time with people who like to and want to win. Lots of folks are going to rain on your parade and tell you, "You can't do that, it's too risky," or shout some other form of fear-mongering at you. You have to be careful who you listen to because even some of the people cheering me on today thought at one time or another that what I was doing was crazy. Why? Because it's not what they personally were comfortable with doing, and they did not fully understand my goals or the level of my determination to reach them. Some of the mindset shifts you will learn to make and embrace are contradictory to much of what you and I were taught in school. The new concepts I was learning to grasp seemed crazy when I first started. [Now that I think of it, maybe the idea of the Kansas City SuperSonics basketball team isn't that far off from a future reality.]

Since you're reading this, then you've already made the decision to take the first step in your journey to becoming a real estate investor. Is it going to be a lot of work? Definitely, but you have to remember your why and be willing to learn as you go. Commit a lot of time as a student, and immerse yourself in reading and listening to experts in the field.

When I started investing in real estate, I had to learn by trial and error. I didn't have a lot of resources to help guide my decisions. But you have the opportunity to learn quickly and take action without making the same mistakes I did. Start by using all the FREE resources available to you through the Troy Kearns Channel on YouTube, TikTok, Instagram, Facebook, Twitter, and my website. I recommend that you check out author Robert Kiyosaki's website, richdad.com, and try to find a Rich Dad's CashFlow club in your area. Seek out other local real estate investment meetups to attend. Join the National Real Estate Investors Association (NREIA https://nationalreia.org); there are different chapters all over the country you can get involved with locally.

I made it a priority to invest in myself when I first started, and I still do. Early on in my quest, I remember going to a Tony Robbins seminar and burning my feet as I walked on the fire while yelling, "Cool moss!" I still am a huge Tony Robbins fan, and it's fun to get pumped up by him, but the best mentors are the people you will connect with at investment clubs, meetups, seminars, and other events that you attend. When I was starting to get involved with the REO (real estate owned by banks, aka foreclosures) business as a real estate agent and attending industry conferences, I had two strategies: Meet as many asset managers as possible, and meet smart agents from other areas (non-competitors) to team up with and share resources.

There are mastermind groups everywhere that you can pay to join - some are worth it, some are not. You will need to do your own due diligence to find the right one(s) that fits your style. Collective Genius is one that I am trying to get into, but they are full to capacity in all the markets I work. This group's membership initiation fee is $25,000, but paying even that much won't get me in the front door. Why do I want in? The answer is that "your network is your net worth," and a lot of the guys I know are involved with Collective Genius. Sometimes you have to look for or create other opportunities. Maybe I'll start my own mastermind group and add people who are in alignment with my direction. Here is a well-known fundamental of success: Success breeds success. You need to surround yourself with like-minded folks who are also trying to get to where you want to be or have already arrived.

Over the years, I have attended seminars featuring speakers such as Bill Clinton, George Bush, Donald Trump, Robert Kiyosaki, and many other famous people and celebrities. These star-studded seminars are great for inspiration, but the relationships I built and the common ground I shared with regular folks from other regions, countries, circumstances, and environmental situations were what really helped me to get ahead.

Today, I am still in contact with many of the professionals I met at professional conferences. At a seminar I attended some years ago for syndicated real estate deals, I was able to share dinner with Tom Wheelwright. Tom is a famous Certified Public Accountant (CPA), author, and a Rich Dad Advisor. Earlier that year, Tom had signed a book for me at another seminar. His teachings had transformed how I invest, and he was someone I greatly respected. And because of our network connection, I found myself having dinner with him. You can bet your bottom dollar I took the time to build a relationship with him while we dined. When you are able to make the possibility become a reality, don't be a wallflower in that situation - be outgoing. Ask good questions of smart people; their answers are a big part of how I got to where I am. Remember the old adage that "Good luck happens when preparation meets opportunity."

Each time you attend a seminar, conference, or mastermind, you will share resources. There are a lot of people way smarter than I am, and each of those people knows smart people, so collectively, they really cut down my learning curve after I meet them in a seminar setting. You can certainly do everything yourself, or you can rely on others who do it better and faster and are willing to teach you how. Not only do you learn what they know, but you usually leave inspired by the teachers. I remember the first time I heard Tony Robbins speak. In 2007, I was at a conference in Chicago featuring Donald Trump as a speaker. Unfortunately, I was unable to see or hear Trump because he was late, and I had to catch a flight. However, before I left, Tony Robbins came out for one hour of power and intensity and just blew my mind. This guy is electric, and when you have him for one whole hour, he's like a bomb detonating inside your head. Guys like Tony will inspire you, and the network you build through masterminds, conferences, and other meetups are invaluable. Getting inspired is also why constantly looking at, tweaking, and adding to your goals is so important. Don't wait until tomorrow or the next day. START RIGHT NOW!

Start writing your goals down, and don't be afraid of them. Write those big, ambitious goals that you think you'll never hit. You can act on a small goal to get some momentum going, but don't procrastinate. The more you push things out, the less likely you are to become successful. There are ways to get started, even without money. You could have a million different excuses as to why you can't start today, but tomorrow isn't guaranteed. Ensure that you are successful today by simply starting. Read this short book, make an action plan, and get to work!

Know your WHY (why you do what you do) and motivate yourself to start NOW.

- Do you want to retire early?
- Do you want to make sure that your family is well taken care of?
- Do you want to create a life you love living?
- You can do all that by investing in real estate. Even having no money to invest isn't a problem as long as you have time to invest.

"A goal is a dream with a deadline."

Napoleon Hill

Make a plan NOW.

You are the only one who can truly answer the following questions and those above.

- What is your strategy to get started TODAY?
- How much money do you have to invest with/can you start with no money?
- How much money do you need each month if you want to retire?
- What are your goals, big and small?
- How much time are you willing to spend each week working towards your goals (not just studying but actively getting started)?
- What skills do you already have that can help you?

A good goal-setting strategy that I have used is to plan daily, weekly, monthly and yearly goals. The goals that you set daily help you hit your weekly goals, and so on. Here's an example of how I lay out my goals:

Health (Why did I start with health? Your body and brain are your two most important personal assets - you have to take good care of them, especially when you're an entrepreneur)

Daily: Weigh yourself daily, make healthy diet choices, keep moving during the day, get 45 minutes of exercise.

Weekly: Do yoga, running, weight training, and something fun like a hiking work-out - minimum five days, aim for six.

Monthly: Run a 5k under 26 minutes; ride a bike 10 miles plus; get to your "10 lbs off" weight, and go swimming a few times.

Yearly: Run a 10k; get to ideal weight and maintain; become flexible enough to do a hand or headstand; get mile run pace under eight minutes; compete in races; get more flexible daily; do more workouts than you miss; try your hardest at everything you do.

This is just a basic example of how you can set goals for yourself using periods of time. Your goals will be different; the main thing is to set them. I also suggest that you incorporate a vision board for the coming year. The vision board should symbolize all your goals as pictures on the board. These boards are powerful because most of us are visual learners to some degree. A few years ago, I showed visually that I wanted to live in three houses in three states so I could easily bounce around the country from key geographic locations. And that goal is currently coming true (Las Vegas, Kansas City, Naples). But when I put it up on the vision board, I was thinking it might be a little bit crazy. I want a jet - it's still there on my vision board. I also want to shoot decent golf, so there's an image of a group of golfers up there. You have to put in the work, but the vision board reminds you of what you want and helps to keep you focused. Goal setting is essentially like a GPS map for your future: If you don't plug in the coordinates, you'll be lost and driving in circles. If you start with goals, you'll have a target that you can see and hit.

Don't set goals that are too extreme and impossible to hit, and don't set goals that are too easy; both will show up as invalid, and you'll know quickly that you need to reset. I have overstated my annual goals in the past. When that happens, I tweak and keep them for the following year. Remember, you have to know where you want to go in order to set a course (goals) to get there. If you're brand new to goal setting, keep it simple and get some victories under your belt. The following is an example of an action plan for somebody like yourself just getting started.

Take Action Now

Daily: Read one chapter of Millionaire Mentorship; watch Troy's Wholesaling video on YouTube.

Weekly: Drive to 50 houses and put them in DealMachine (see link on page 13) follow up with all leads via phone and text; read Troy's Wholesaling Contract form on www.troykearnschannel.com and fill out a sample.

Monthly: Get first wholesale deal under contract; build buyers list; create a website for business.

Yearly: Complete eight wholesale deals, buy two rental properties, save 20% of net income, pay off credit card debt.

Before you continue to Chapter Two, take 15 minutes and write down the immediate goals you have.

I recommend that you categorize your goals into Finance, Personal, Family, Health, BIG GOALS, or whichever categories fit you best. It's not just about money, though that's usually the most immediate need. [If you feel you're overweight, you could consider addressing that because it may be on your mind as part of a success/failure mindset.]

This is the start of one of my favorite hikes, located on the Kraft Mountain Loop outside Las Vegas. Come on, take that first step on your journey into real estate investing. YOU can do this!

CHAPTER

TWO

What Type of Investor Are You Going to Be?

THIS DEPENDS ON where you're at in life. Your financial situation is going to determine how you start out as an investor. What are your needs? Are you willing to take risks? Let me be clear: It's not risky to invest in real estate, but in general, some investments in real estate are risky, such as vacant apartment buildings or fire-damaged flips. Avoid risk and mitigate risk, but also understand that some risk is OK, but it's not OK just to make risky decisions.

Do you lack savings and have a pile of debt? Or are you on the opposite end of the scale and have lots of money, but you don't know where to start? Most people aren't either, but more likely somewhere in between.

If you're 18 years old or younger and reading this book, you might not have any money to invest, but maybe you've got a lot of time. Maybe you don't have as much time, but you have some savings and a good credit score and wonder what your investment options are. Regardless of whether or not you're broke or somewhere in-between, hunting for deals as an entry-level investor is the best place to start. It will teach you the basics of investing in real estate. Hunting for deals means driving around and looking for vital signs of properties, which we'll get into later.

A little more info about each type:

Wholesaler, aka The Middle Man

When I first started investing, I didn't understand wholesaling. If you're thinking, "What the heck is wholesaling?" you're not alone. The short answer is this: The wholesaler contracts the home with a buyer at a higher price than with the seller and keeps the difference as profit. Real estate wholesalers generally find and contract distressed properties. You act as a middle man without having to take money out of your own pocket to make a deal. This is the same method our first Millionaire Mentorship contest winner, Joel Palacios of Houston, Texas, got started with in real estate investing. [Don't forget to check my YouTube channel and social media often for announcements about the next Millionaire Mentorship contest. If you're just starting out, you could win and an opportunity to work directly with me in your area as we flip a house together. The history of my partnership with Joel is also available to you on my YouTube

Joel Palacios, winner of the first Millionaire Mentorship contest, meeting with me outside the home we are flipping together in Houston, TX. Joel started out in real estate investment as a wholesaler.

Channel, TikTok, Instagram, and Facebook. Remember - you have to enter to win the Millionaire Mentorship contest!]

No matter where you are in life, wholesaling is the best way to start to learn real estate investing with the least amount of risk! When you don't have money to invest, but you've got some time on your hands, this is the best way to go, especially for young people with no college opportunities on the horizon. Here's what you can do right now without a real estate license:

- The best way to search for and record distressed properties while on the road is to register for the DealMachine app on your mobile device (https://dealmachine.app.link/troy). DealMachine is the highest-rated real estate investor software because it's cost-effective, efficient and allows you to work individually or as part of a team. Driving for dollars is the term used when you drive around a neighborhood that you think could house future wholesale deals, then document distressed properties with your mobile device to create unique lead lists. DealMachine is a more direct, much faster approach to finding wholesale properties than simply sending out emails to inboxes or letters in the mail. Consider this: From your car, you can find a property, photograph it and locate it in the local tax assessor records. Then, you have the option of calling the owner immediately or mailing a letter of interest to the owner later. I cannot emphasize enough how great this app is for beginning wholesalers! [If you use the link above to sign up for my DealMachine app, you will receive a 7 day free trial and $15 free credit which could be used for 25 postcards or 100 free skip traces.]

- Find a good deal on a property and make the seller/owner an offer (get the property under contract - we have sample contracts on www.troykearnschannel.com).
- Find a buyer for the property and assign the contract to the buyer.
- Take the profit from the difference between your offer to the seller and the amount paid by the buyer.
- Set up a Real Estate Investment bank account and deposit the profit to use for future investing.

Wholesaling has become a lot more popular in the last five to seven years because its inherent low risk has attracted social media influencers who are now selling courses online. The word "wholesale" brings to mind someone getting a good deal if they are able to buy something at a wholesale price (what a retail vendor would pay). In real estate, the term describes locking down property with a contract at a discounted price and then selling the rights to the contract to a buyer, usually an investor.

I got my start wholesaling properties and flipping properties in 2012-13. I was already finding deals and flipping but hadn't personally wholesaled any properties because I was buying all my deals in Las Vegas. I was unfamiliar with the wholesaling process and did not have a wholesale buyer's list, but in general, I thought that wholesaling in Nevada as a licensed realtor was a bad idea. Wholesaling in the state where you're licensed creates a lot of disclosure issues based on conflicts of interest. Even when you do the required disclosures, you could risk angering a seller who may report you to the state Real Estate Division for further investigation. Top Tip:

Don't do wholesaling in the state where you are a licensed realtor. Following this rule has kept me out of hot water.

In 2013, I was a groomsman at a friend's wedding in New Orleans. That friend introduced me to Chris, one of the other groomsmen. Chris and I talked all wedding weekend about real estate, and I learned that he had gone full-tilt side hustle flipping and wholesaling in hopes of replacing the income from his medical sales job that he wanted to leave. Chris and I started working together a lot in 2013-2015, and during that time, we wholesaled lots of properties. The reason we were able to do so many is that New Orleans was just starting to recover from Hurricane Katrina, which smashed and inundated the great "Big Easy" in 2005. A lot of residents just left their homes and moved out of town for good. There were vacant and abandoned properties everywhere in New Orleans. Having spent pretty much all of my career on the ultra-high-cost West Coast, this was exciting. Moreover, the spread (profit) on these properties was huge: $50-100,000 plus in potential profit on each deal. Wholesaling deals like this were easy in NOLA (New Orleans, Louisiana), and Chris was able to build up a very solid buyer's list.

Chris and I really started to build something big in NOLA. We formally partnered in the wholesaling business: I would make all the calls from Vegas, and Chris would go to the appointments, or we would go together when I was in town and close the deals. Together, we sold dozens of properties and made very big money on several!

Let me tell you about a couple of deals for which we sold wholesale contracts. One of our largest paydays was an old large brick structure built in the 1800s, with historical "slave quarters" in the back, which tells you about how old it actually was. The property was on the verge of collapse, barely standing. The lady who originally bought the property had planned to renovate it, but she passed away unexpectedly, and her sister, who lived out of state, was left to deal with the property. She had many offers and a lot of interest in the property, but I built a lot of rapport with her. Top Tip: One of the things that you need to know as a wholesaler is that the rapport you build with your sellers can be gone in an instant if the buyer you bring to the table screws up the deal. Make sure you work with people who will not damage your reputation.

On this particular deal, we were able to get it under contract for around $1.4 million dollars. We found a major developer who was going to turn the property into town homes or apartments. We closed the sale and made almost $100,000 gross profit. We divided up $90,000 after expenses, and everyone was happy. The seller was happy because we facilitated the transaction and did what we said. The buyer/developer was happy because they would not have found that deal without us; at that time, wholesale deals were sent directly to the buyers and not advertised everywhere. [Obviously, things have changed a bit since, and now Facebook groups are very popular for advertising wholesale deals.] That was one of many wholesale deals we did. As we transitioned into more flipping than wholesaling, we effectively closed down our wholesaling business because we stopped working on it.

Today, Chris and I own quite a few properties together in New Orleans, as well as several other properties in other states. He is now developing large storage facilities, building new homes, and is very active in the short-term rental market. I am making large commercial acquisitions and flipping like gangbusters, as well as working on a million other things. My point here is that wholesaling teaches you the fundamentals of real estate: In other words, you look to find a property under market value; learn how to come up with the improved or fixed-up value of it when sold, as well as the actual cost to fix it; and calculate the profit. Seasoned investors will tell you that you make money when you buy, not when you sell. Wholesaling teaches you how to buy right. Let me talk a bit more about that.

What's the formula for a good deal? That's a great question, so let's break it down into specifics. The rule of thumb across the country is that you should buy improved property at 65% of ARV. ARV, or After Repair Value, is the market (selling price). The true working formula is this: 65% of ARV minus repairs. [This key formula will be utilized again in a later chapter to reinforce your knowledge.]

Let's say you are looking at a property to buy. The ARV or market value is $300,000, but it needs a cosmetic upgrade that is going to cost you $40,000. You should buy that property for $155,000, a price which is arrived at with this calculation: 65% of $300,000 = $195,000 - $40,000 = $155,000. Will you make a $105,000 profit? No, because you have expenses that have to be deducted. Holding costs, commissions, and negotiation fees will eat up at least 5-8% of your total sales price, so you get the point.

Now, there are some markets you can buy at a higher ARV, and I'll explain why. If you have newer homes with fast (few) Days on Market (DOM) (meaning houses are selling fast) and there is a low supply, you can afford to come up on the percentage. For example, in Vegas, I don't stick to the 65% ARV number because the days on market are so fast, and deals generally are easy "fix & flips." More importantly, if you stick to the 65% ARV rule in Vegas, you'll never get a deal to work because they may not exist. In Kansas City, I might buy a property for 50% of ARV or less, but the work and time needed to fix it would be much more and generally take a lot longer. The 65% of ARV is a guideline, but obviously, the more lucrative a deal you can get for yourself, the better.

You can structure wholesale pricing for all types of deals; they don't have to be just flips. I recently bought a property at 100% of ARV, or at full market, because the terms were so good. This pricing strategy also works great when discussing taking over properties subject to or with creative financing.

I want to share another story about wholesaling with you. In 2013, I was heavily involved in wholesaling and reinventing myself as a flipper. I decided that it would be a good idea to learn more about flipping from the best or what I thought was the best. I bought a franchise from HomeVestors, commonly known as We Buy Ugly Houses. This franchise works for a lot of people I know personally, but my experience was not the same. Basically, I felt franchisees were pooling our money together to buy leads. On top of that, a lot of those leads were garbage, and I didn't get very many of those! In fact, I didn't do much business at all as the owner of the franchise, so I returned the franchise rights and went back to doing it myself. Why am I telling you this? I don't believe this franchise has a lot of added value. When you buy into a franchise, you are buying into a name and a system. HomeVestors has the name, but the system was outdated when I was a franchisee, and leadership didn't seem interested in elevating or updating their technology or media presence. However, I did get to meet a lot of cool individuals. Many people love franchises, but I learned that I don't particularly like being told what I can and cannot do in my business by anyone other than the government powers that be. My recommendation to you is not to start with a franchise. If you are looking to get into wholesaling, simply go to my YouTube Channel and check out our videos on wholesaling. We are constantly updating and improving our presentations, and you get to ask questions directly, as well as request content you'd like to see.

If you're brand new and/or nervous about starting out, wholesaling is a way that you can use your skip tracing research skills (skip tracing in real estate is the process of locating the owner of a property) and phone to track down people in real-time and get their property under contract. It really is the best way to start out your investing path without having to worry about losing your own money. You also get to watch other flippers and observe their successes and failures. I have heard some would-be investors say, "I don't want to call people because I don't like it." To be successful, sometimes you need to do things that you don't like. I do not like doing paperwork, but in the beginning, I had to do it! The staff does the paperwork for me now. As you become more and more successful, you will be able to delegate the little things you do not like to do. Use the thought of that as a motivator to reach success quickly through extra effort.

The First-Time Flipper

My first flip was a property I bought in 2004 as my second house. It was a live-in flip. The house was located in the Renton Highlands in Washington State and was not habitable. My agent and mentor Arron had shown me lots of deals, but we settled on finding a property that I could buy and then fix while I lived in it. Looking back, I can't believe the bank financed me.

I wanted to learn how to do all the work and fix up the whole house by myself. I had zero experience with or knowledge of construction, but I wanted to learn. My uncle was a contractor and offered to help me. I told him I wanted to learn the complete process. He had me pay him to make me do the work, so it was a good deal for the both of us (maybe a tad better for him). I sweated copper, did miter cuts, painted the interior and exterior, installed all new doors, and replaced the flooring everywhere in the house. One of my best memories is building the deck with my best friend, Travis. We were in our early 20s, out of college, working and living together. We had a lot of fun laying out the deck and putting in each screw. The process of building that deck with my best friend is still one of my fondest memories. It was a small project, but we learned a lot, especially how to work together to complete something that neither one of us had ever done before. For example, we used ironwood for the planking, which required us to predrill each hole before screwing the plank to the base. After the house renovations were finally completed and I had given my uncle his final payment, two things came into focus: I really learned a lot about the construction process, and I never wanted to do that work again. Still, I gained the knowledge needed to become a good flipper, and that helped me immeasurably in the future to come.

That first house flip had a lot of great memories, not only because I did all the work (with some help) but also because I house-hacked it. In the beginning of my real estate investing, I always rented out empty bedrooms in the properties I bought. It just seemed silly to keep an otherwise empty room with stuff in it when that room could offer income and a cool way to have roommates with common goals. This concept might be something for you to consider as a way of offsetting expenses when you're first getting started.

I really didn't start flipping full time until eight years later! [The first one must have really worn me out - just kidding.] I really wish I had continued flipping, but bad investments in Las Vegas led me down a different trail. It would take some time, but I returned to this solid investment method and restarted flipping in 2012. By then, I had done a lot of rental renovations on cheap properties I bought in Las Vegas from 2009-2011 and had been working with a good contractor. Things were slowing down for me in real estate sales, so I was looking for other income sources. I was laser-focused on acquiring properties, which ended up being the better long-term move, but flippers crushed it during the downturn in Vegas. They were buying in an economy that was unpredictable by outsiders but very predictable to the flippers. They knew the market was going down, but a real estate sales cycle is not as fast as stocks, so you have some time. A friend of mine, Jared Weiss (who recently passed away at a very young age of 49), was a flipper at the time. He flipped thousands of houses and made hundreds of millions of dollars. He was a master of markets too, as you will learn.

In 2011, due to rampant financial fraud, Nevada passed a law to make it a criminal offense for banks to foreclose on a property without following a mandated legal procedure. The enactment of this law basically caused all pending foreclosures to come to a screeching halt. Upon learning of the law's implementation, my flipper friend Jared loaded up with every short sale he could find on the market. [A short sale in real estate is one in which a house is sold for a price that is less than the amount still owed on the mortgage.]

Before the new foreclosure law's passage, short sales could take years to close and would often fall through before a deal was reached. As a result, a lot of agents just didn't know about or want to deal with the process, which also was constantly changing. At the same time, foreclosures could be bought with no hassle. However, because of the disruptions caused by the massive real estate crash, banks were going under and being bought, so it was a messy time. When all foreclosures stopped in their tracks, the short sale market skyrocketed, and Jared already had everything under contract. It was a brilliant move, and I learned a lot from watching him. He had almost no risk, just his earnest money. Jared saw all that would occur before it happened and locked down the whole market. Everyone tried to follow, but he had such a big lead that it made him a monster. RIP Jared Weiss.

The example above is why you must learn to understand market timing in the world of real estate. The timing there is constantly changing, much like the tide. If you're in the water (real estate market) and not looking around, you could get swallowed up by a big wave. The key to flipping is to turn your money as fast as possible versus making the most per deal. If you make $40,000 per deal, but you repeat three times per year, that's $120,000. It might take a year or more for the flipper who is trying to make $100,000 on one deal, but in a period that long, the market could get better, or it might get worse. The bigger the deal over time, the bigger the risk.

Here's the most important thing that you need to take away if you are brand new to real estate and flipping properties: Start with the easy ones. Don't take on the big jobs. Flip the properties that just need new paint, carpet, flooring, and maybe some appliances. Take on those you could finish yourself, if you had to, in the shortest amount of time. You don't need to get in over your head too quickly; you just want to be able to take calculated risks. Now, if you're a flipper, but you also grew up with a hammer in your hand, and you can fix the entire property, it's entirely different. In my opinion, though, you still should plan on not taking longer than six weeks to complete your first rehab, and in the best scenario, you should have it sold within 90-120 days. Remember, the flipping game is about turning your money quickly. Get in, get out, repeat, and learn by doing in greater volume. As with anything, fundamentals are the first thing you need to learn; then you need repetition to become proficient. Start with the easy layups, but sell the hard ones for a fee to a bigger player. That way, you will live to fight another day, and you can work those hard ones later as you become more successful. Trust me, they are all sorts of fun, but they come with too much risk for a newbie.

Let's say you've established good credit, have some money to invest (or have a lender), and you're ready to get some skin in the game and maybe put in a little sweat equity, too. Here are a few things you can start right away.

- You can spend your free time searching for houses online and on the road.
- Learn to understand which repairs bring the most value without overspending. YouTube is a great resource for learning about repairs and their costs. After you've viewed my channel for the latest video, do a search and check out how to replace a vanity or a kitchen sink, or a carpet...
- Research and understand the local market to make sure an

improved prospective property could sell/rent quickly at the pricing you establish.

When you find a property that you can afford, don't hesitate. Make the call and set things in motion.

The Sophisticated Investor

As you grow in investing, you will find that learning a new vocabulary comes with your new endeavor. [Sidebar: I encourage you to add the Glossary link at the back of this book to your web favorites, so you can quickly find the meaning of real estate terms you do not currently understand.] Commercial real estate can be difficult to grasp at times because of some confusing terminology used in that sector. For example, Triple Net is a phrase that you used to hear fairly often. A triple net lease (triple-net or NNN) is a type of lease agreement on a property whereby the tenant or lessee promises to pay all the expenses of the property, including 1) real estate taxes, 2) building insurance, and 3) maintenance. Pretty straightforward, right? The "New and Improved" replacement term is Common Area Maintenance or CAM, which is where landlords identify and list all the property expenses that they pass onto tenants, aka Triple Net and even more! There will be many examples of new terms and words that challenge you along your path, but it's just part of the process that we go through when learning anything new.

Two terms that are occasionally used interchangeably to describe a type of investor are "Accredited Investor" and "Sophisticated Investor." Although the case could be made that there is some overlap, these two terms are quite different in meaning, and it is a mistake to trade one term for the other.

An accredited investor is an individual or entity that meets specific requirements based on Securities Exchange Commission (SEC) guidelines to participate in Regulation D offerings for raising large capital. The SEC conceived the term and created this category to promote private offerings while still making them safe and secure. To be considered an accredited investor, you are required to meet one of the following standards:

- You are an individual with a net worth (spousal worth allowed) of more than $1 million, excluding your primary residence.

- In each of the last two years, you have had an individual income in excess of $200,000; or a joint income (with a spouse) in excess of $300,000 and expect to continue to attain that income level.

As of August 2020, the SEC also defined measures of professional knowledge, experience, or certifications for accredited investors. Additionally, the SEC has opened up the possibility of more professional licenses being added in the future.

A sophisticated investor is likely to have a very high net worth and/or high income. Additionally, a sophisticated investor is expected to have highly developed investment and financial knowledge and great investment intuition in order to make sound investment and financial decisions. A sophisticated investor is constantly researching the economy and financial markets and thoroughly understands any investment situation before making a decision on how to invest. Additionally, they have the resources to withstand a financial loss if an investment turns negative. The sophisticated investor does not have the formal requirements of an accredited investor. Sometimes SEC regulations require that investors be accredited because they are presumed to be able to handle the risk, as are sophisticated investors. Both are sought after for large capital projects, such as professional sports stadiums or arenas or real estate syndications. [Real estate syndication (or property syndication) is a partnership among several investors. The investors combine their skills, resources, and capital to purchase and manage a property they otherwise couldn't afford.]

Real estate has so many ways for you to make money that the longer you are in the game, the more opportunities you will have, such as:

- Historical Tax Credit Financing
- Purchasing a property that qualifies for tax credits, then selling the property and your tax credits, making a profit on both
- A lease where you partner with the tenant in their success
- Perhaps the state is willing to probate your taxes. Maybe the state will even cut you in on a piece of the sales tax of a big project.
- None of this is far-fetched. Take a look at any NFL stadium - the chances are that you have helped fund some billionaire sports franchise through levied tax dollars.

You can stay in your lane, of course, and make as much as hundreds of millions of dollars buying valuable properties through a handful of ways, never even having to leave your home. Real estate truly has endless possibilities. But please try to understand; just being labeled something doesn't make you something. If it sounds too easy, it's not, and if it sounds hard, it's probably got money or something rewarding behind it. The more investing you do, the easier it becomes.

If you are a sophisticated investor, you are long in your journey, but maybe you could use a little extra boost. Maybe you are further along than I am, but because your journey was different, you are now reading this book to get educated and excited about different things. I hope that my perspective will help you grow in your investments.

Even if you are a sophisticated investor, you need to challenge yourself. Currently, I am working on buying a large building in downtown Kansas City. It carries a big price tag, and I am solo on the deal. People tend to like partnerships in business because they spread the risk. Even though I have many partnerships, I prefer to roll solo on a lot of things. [My wife refers to me as a lone wolf.] Partnerships are great and can work very well when there is good chemistry among partners. Here's a side note on a partnership that worked well for me. When I first got started selling REO properties, I blew up like crazy. Meaning that I was such a good sales person, I talked my way into working with more banks than I could handle or really had the experience to work properly. My broker and team lead, now my friend Iddo, became a great partner, and we made lots of money together. At that time, I was splitting all my earned commissions with Iddo: 65% to me and 35% to Iddo. So if one of my deals brought $10,000 in commission, I would get $6,500, and Iddo would be paid $3,500. We had the perfect symbiotic relationship: I was a prodigious rainmaker who didn't have the money to pay for overhead then, and Iddo had an established business to administer the details of the thousands of deals that I ran through his office. He was happy to pay for all of the office staff expenses, with the exception of my assistant. He also paid for all the bank's expenses, including rekeying doors, utilities, and trashouts (taking the trash out of abandoned or foreclosed homes to prepare them for resale). I had some people tell me that my split with Iddo was not such a great deal for me, but from my perspective, I have no complaints. After all, I received 65% net of the total commission on every deal and had no worries about employees, bookkeeping, accounting, or outlay of hundreds of thousands of dollars! Even when I did have the money, I preferred buying properties versus floating money for the bank. So that is exactly what I did, and it worked out great for me. If you and your partner are happy with a partnership, it's a good partnership, even if others don't like it. By the way, Iddo loved our partnership. Who wouldn't? One guy brings in thousands of deals, and after paying the overhead spread out over all those deals, it's pure profit to Iddo!

I have had partnerships where I did not get a fair deal, and those ended. Currently, I own close to 60 doors (rental properties) with another business partner. John and I have a great partnership. We have built up a rock-solid trust: He looks out for me, and I look out for him. He also has other partners that he invests with, and so do I, but we make a lot of investments together. Sometimes I will want to take bigger risks than John. That is good too because if I feel strongly about something and he doesn't want in, our relationship is such that I could buy it myself or find another partner. Business partnerships are just like personal relationships; trust and time will make them strong or weak, based on how much time and energy you invest in them. John and I started as partners in his REO business. We grew it together, I consulted with him, and we rolled that relationship and money into buying homes. We are now in the process of building homes near each other in Florida. We started working together almost 13 years ago, and now both of us don't have to work. When we started, we were far away from that accomplishment. John and I work extremely well together, and because of that, we are able to share our lives and families together, go on vacations together, and learn together. "La dolce vita" – it's a very sweet life right now.

I am thankful for all of the partnerships that I have had and look forward to more. Find someone with a skill set that you don't have - that is one of the key things that make a good partnership!

Sophisticated investors have accountants, lawyers, tax strategists, and business consultants, and they are constantly modifying their craft and upgrading their portfolio. I admire super-sophisticated guys like Stephen Ross, the gigantic developer from New York who owns the Miami Dolphins - he's really an amazing guy. My goal is to be somewhat like him or maybe Carl Icahn, another sophisticated real estate investor, who is more of a corporate raider type; Icahn has had some huge real estate deals, such as buying the foreclosed Fontainebleau Las Vegas and flipping it for close to a $500 million dollar profit. Remember, if you are the smartest person in the room, those aren't bragging rights; that's the time to invite some smarter people in the room or move to another room. You have to think differently to get ahead, and smart people think differently.

- Start by looking for large multi-unit properties
- Hire a lawyer who specializes in real estate
- Become knowledgeable, so you don't get cheated or defrauded
- Seek like-minded and knowledgeable partners

CHAPTER

THREE

How Much Money do you Need to Retire?

SOONER OR LATER, we all ask that question. Most people retire when they are past their prime, and all their prime time was eaten up working for someone else. You don't have to do it that way if you invest in real estate.

As you achieve financial freedom with investing, your goals will change. Just keep in mind that once you hit your first target, you should move your target to grow even more. I am now working on writing this book, but I am, by definition, retired. In other words, if I want to hang it up right now, I could shut everything down and live the life of leisure, but I want to accomplish more. This personal goal change is not for everybody, and that's OK. I have lots of friends who are saying, "Yep, I am fishing." Good for them - it's just not for me right now.

It comes down to how you want to live. Take a moment to think about the word WEALTH.

I'd like you to look at the practical definition of being wealthy. Wealthy simply means not having to work but still being able to spend the same amount of money you spent yesterday, while having more to spend tomorrow. This kind of wealth is achieved through setting up a stream of passive income, which is earned with little or no effort; having a rental house is one example. Active income means you have to be actively involved in your business in order to produce money. Which one sounds better to you?

In order to build wealth and be able to retire with passive income, you first have to figure out how much money you need. You might live in a small town where it's very cheap to live, and you don't have many expenses, or you might live in a big city with a lavish lifestyle and want to own islands in the Bahamas. Whichever lifestyle you want for retirement, it's possible through real estate. You just have to determine how much you need to retire.

When I first started, I was 23, single and fresh out of college, trying to find myself. I knew I wanted to be rich, but I thought it was going to be through the stock market. At 17 years old, I started investing in mutual funds because I read a book called "The Wealthy Barber" by David Chilton. It was sort of a "save and invest in mutual funds" book. I didn't think I was that smart to become an investor, but I knew I could outwork just about anyone. I have always been very competitive with work at jobs and other roles and did well, for the most part, moving up in the job market. The bottom line is that I was a student fresh out of college and had zero direction other than finding a way to get what I wanted, which was financial independence, and that meant I wanted to be rich. My parents were great at raising us kids, but we grew up poor, by most standards. I did not miss out on the most basic things, but my parents struggled, and we were definitely not spoiled. I always felt I had to earn what I wanted from a very young age. Struggle makes you strong. Not having a lot of money motivated me to work hard, and I consider my work ethic to be one of my best strengths to this day.

My point is this: I was determined but uneducated. The tools available then to track down a house to flip were far less than they are today. Back in the day, you might spend hours at the county courthouse flipping through microfilm reels or, worse, poring over paper records to find the owner of a property. There were no apps on your phone to send an email directly to a person, and then do a skip trace and call them on the spot; load them in your CRM (customer relationship management app), and then go to "YouTube University" and figure out how to close them. There were blogs, there were books, and there were seminars and trade shows. But the multitude of videos (on every imaginable subject) you can get through YouTube, along with selective repetition on-demand, as well as the sheer volume of advanced software on the computer and personal devices, are huge boons for learning and doing. Combining those on-the-ground educational advances with instantly accessible county and city tax data makes it so much easier for you to get started today.

As I look toward the future, I have some ambitious goals that I never thought I would set. I also have some practical investing strategies. As I get older, I am more interested in tax liens, large development, private-public partnerships, grant programs for HUD housing, subdivisions, and more. In my life now, I can afford to take more risks because I know far more than when I was younger. I know how to use my time, energy, and money wisely and how to stay away from people or things that suck those things away from me. I can tell which investment is probably going to be a loser, but if it's a calculated risk where something can be learned from the investment, and I make money, great. I know that always having multiple exit strategies on any investment is the most critical thing to survival in rough waters, and being determined to make it work no matter what happens is the best attitude.

Step into real estate investing as if it were your first time running. Don't try to run a marathon out of the gate. However, set your goal to run that marathon eventually, and once you have that down, improve on the process (time) and then move the goal to your next projected mark. The best thing about real estate is that you get to determine where the end is.

I have been a quasi runner for a long time. I would run the occasional 5k, half marathon, jog on and off, here and there. Let's be honest - it's hard to really like running up until you get good at it, then it's more bearable. When you're an on and off runner, you never get anywhere fast, literally. However, once you focus, really study, and act by using the right method, it's a whole new ball game. Stretch correctly by warming up first with light exercise, then do your stretching. Mentally focus, breathe properly and take running seriously as an actual sport. At age 44, I am running longer and faster than I ever have, but it's only because I focused on getting better and taking the right steps, with the realization that I couldn't become a good runner overnight. I learned that I need to condition with short runs daily and get in a good (5k or longer) run weekly. Once I started that regimen, running became easier, and I got faster and stronger. I still have a long way to go; and let's not forget, I have the time since I don't have the job excuse. :)

Maybe you just want to chill, play golf, watch TV, or go live in the woods off the grid, but make $10,000 per month passively. All that is possible, and your goals will change as you grow but start today. Start now, don't wait - time is on your side with starting, but not if you keep procrastinating.

What is the total cost of your monthly expenses?

1. How much do you currently have to pay for bills each month?

2. How much do you spend on the fun stuff? Make sure you take this seriously. Cut the fat! If you're overspending today, then success tomorrow is going to be harder for you to see. Invest in yourself by making sure you cut costly personal expenses and habits because they will cost you the time and money that you need to succeed in investing. There is an old expression that is very applicable: "Rich people stay rich by living like they're broke. Broke people stay broke by living like they're rich."

You need food, water, clothing, and shelter. All the rest are choices. If you're young and single when you start out investing, you can rent out rooms in the first house you purchase and use that rental money to pay for extra expenses. This is an example of how every buying decision I make has one universal concept behind it: Someone else is going to pay for it. What do I mean? When I buy a car, no matter what the payment is, I will buy a house that I can rent to make that payment. In effect, the tenants are going to pay for my car. Think about that for a while; it took me a long time to get the idea. Let's say you buy a house, and the rental income is $500. You then buy a car with a $500 monthly payment. Although you write the check for the car, who is actually paying for it? You invested, and your investment, by way of your tenants, pays for the car. Once the car is paid off, you will still have $500 passive income every month.

Once you are investing, every buying decision should be preceded with the question, "Who's paying for this?" If the answer now is YOU, then it's time for YOU to get started investing because it doesn't have to be YOU doing the paying. This new way of looking at paying for things can be applied across the board, including your mortgage on the home you inhabit. Tenants will pay your mortgage, and once it's paid off, they will be providing you with passive income to use as you wish. The more houses you have, the more real estate you have that produces passive income to pay down debt, decrease taxes and invest. What stock pays a $500 a month dividend on borrowed money, lets you depreciate it, and can be turned into an Airbnb? No stock investment in the known universe has all those benefits. The <u>only</u> investment that does is real estate!

3. Now imagine the life you really want to live. [If you write it down, you will imprint it on your mind.] How much more per month do you need to make?

Dream BIG and put your plan of action together. The whole point of retirement is being able to enjoy it!

If you're 50 years old or older, this could offend you, but bear in mind I am a motivator. If you've been at the job 10, 15, 20, 25 years and you're still chasing that retirement or pension, or 401K, aka the Golden Handcuffs, it's not too late to make a sea change. You don't want to retire old and tired, with your best years behind you. You want to be as young as you can, as fast as you can, with a great plan out in front of you. That is why you are reading this book because you are smart, and you are making a decision to educate yourself about what you don't know. Taking action is the key to success. Overcoming failure and understanding the reasons for failing teach you quickly, while an advanced education costs a whole lot of money that may take years to repay and teaches you pretty slowly.

When I first started investing, I did it all wrong - bought a condo, lost money every month. The next property was a live-in flip. Good for experience, worked out OK, but I had no idea what I was doing, no plan. Then I bought two houses in Vegas on speculation. Oops...

My mentor at the time advised me not to do it. "Rich Dad, Poor Dad," which I had recently read, said don't do it, but I thought I had the casino "figured out." [There are cab drivers in Las Vegas who figured out slot poker but are now too broke to leave the city or cab driving, and all their formerly valuable world possessions are being held for them by the Pawn Stars.] My cousin lived in Vegas. Because I was a "Real Estate Investor," he called to tell me the Vegas real estate market was going up like crazy. The local newspaper said the same thing, and the realtor who sold me the houses also said the same thing, "Who cares if you're losing money every month if it's going up by more in equity?"

Well, when the bottom drops out, and your investments cost you $2,500 per month in cash flow, you live on your cousin's couch and realize what a big mistake you have made. That mistake was not the only teacher in that experience. I also had to figure out how to come out of my dive without foreclosing and screwing up my credit. Let me tell you; I was hanging on for dear life. I had to relocate back to Seattle for ten months, and fortunately, my former boss allowed me to take up my old job. I moved back into my mentor Arron's basement and started all over, just so I could pay for someone else to live in a brand new home I bought in Las Vegas!

Solving those problems and then only buying properties that have positive cash flow were the big takeaways. Learning how to build a real estate empire properly, one house at a time has taught me two things: Time is on your side with real estate. Both houses I bought in Vegas are now worth much more than what I paid for them; and the lessons I learned through the stress and hardship educated me quickly. Once I realized my mistake, I would never be that same investor, and I would never again speculate unless I was OK with losing the money!

Each mistake I made was because I ignored the fundamental principles of good real estate investment. The simple steps that I lay out for you will allow you to become rich, so you can live the most amazing life, one house at a time. You don't have to be smart, young, or old; just take action. Retiring to do whatever you desire whenever you want, and with your capabilities still intact, is what I am talking about. Five years or less is all you need, and you will probably have to quit your full-time job to do it. But you'll start making money and living a better life right away. You certainly can retire in five years if you really work your plan. And believe me, you will be happy that you made the change.

CHAPTER

FOUR

How Do You Buy with No Money Down?

FIRST OF ALL, buying with "no money down" is misleading. When I started out, there were not as many hard money lenders as there are now. Then, no money down meant creative seller financing, where if you found the perfect seller, you could get a deal with no money out of your pocket. Generally, in that scenario, you would have to find a distressed deal and work it out to pay the seller after you stabilized the property. Sometimes you could even get a credit from the seller and get cash at closing, but that is really old school.

A hard money lender determines the value of the property through a BPO (broker price opinion) or an independent appraisal done by a licensed appraiser in the state in which the property is located. The interest rates on hard money loans are typically higher than the rates charged for traditional business loans because they are riskier. Today, there are many hard money lenders and private lenders easily found in every market who will loan you up to 100 percent of the financing. However, those hard money interest rates are not the best (you should do some research on the origination of hard money to get a fuller understanding).

If you have no money to put down, you need to think about how you can make it work without getting skinned. Money is actually the easiest part of real estate investment. Advanced investors understand that. Finding the right deals and quality construction crews are the hard parts to put together. Finding the right deal is truly the hardest part of those two, but you can lose big if you hire the wrong contractor to do the job.

The massive number of hard money lenders, combined with freely available credit on the web, can allow you to borrow to bridge the gap when needed. Effectively, you take zero money out of your pocket and still have the capital for other things (but just to remind, you do borrow it). Buying with no money down is an excellent strategy but not always realistic. What is realistic, and what I try to do, is to buy with less money down, less interest, and over longer-term. Be open to all things in real estate. Something that may have value to you may have no value to others, so that presents an opportunity to negotiate. A definition I like is: Value is derived from knowledge matched with effort, and that equals money!

If you focus only on no money down deals, you could spend a lot of time going nowhere, particularly during the time that you are an unknown in the market. Instead, consider the numerous creative buying strategies available to you, including buying with as little down as possible. Think about how you want to negotiate a price on a deal that optimizes cash flow while you determine your exit strategies and examine how the deal fits into your short and long-term plans.

Now that I have sufficiently cautioned you about seeking no money down deals, I must confess that I have done quite a few. That's because I am a known and trustworthy investor, a reputation that takes time to establish. But I do realize that you will be in that category in the future, so my stories will help to prepare you when an opportunity is in front of you.

One no money down deal we still own is in New Orleans, Louisiana. In 2013, the house was in bad shape, the owner owed $48,000 in taxes, and the property had not sold at the tax sale. The city had not foreclosed on it yet, and no one had bought it. My partner knew the area on which the property was located had changed for the better and now commanded a higher dollar. The bank would loan us the money to fix it, plus give us some money for the equity after the house was repaired. This method today is commonly referred to as BRRRR (Buy, Rehab, Rent, Refinance, Repeat - more on this in Chapter Seventeen). We used to call it cash-out refinance. The owner could have fixed up the property or tried to sell it, but he effectively had let it go 20 years before. When I called him, he said, "Look, I want out of this property, my name taken off the title, and to have nothing further to do with it. I am tired of getting mail from the city, so you can have it. I am too old to deal with it and don't need the money." I responded, "Where would you like me to send the paperwork?" We still own the house to this day. We fixed it up and have rented it out continuously ever since. We have about $200,000 in equity and are considering doing a 1031 exchange with it right now. My partner is a full-blown storage space developer, and I am working on many different projects, as well as trying to find us a storage development to do together. Real estate grows exponentially. If you set it and forget it, years will go by, and one day you'll lift up your head and have a bunch of equity. My partner and I are both conservative, so our money sits in our property until the right opportunity presents itself. It's passive income, so we don't need to manage it, and the cash is set aside for the partnership. Think about that deal:

We bought it with no money, and it's been sitting there, putting cash in the bank. We have not done anything in eight years, and now it's worth $200,000 more than we "didn't pay for it." Plus, we have put tens of thousands of dollars in the bank from equity on the money we did not invest. That example alone proves the enormous power of real estate.

Today, buying with no money down means you need to have excellent credit or a great source of private lenders and a great deal source. Ideally, you want to have both. If you go into real estate investing to grow wealth, you need the ability to borrow. If you have bad credit, it means you ignore your obligations or don't handle your credit issues. Either way, you need to understand your situation and learn how to fix and control it. Find a good lender and learn from local bankers who are smart and share knowledge. Borrowing is key to growing. Understanding good debt and how lending works can keep you from ever having to use your own money as you build your business. [Putting deals together is usually the best way to ensure someone else will pay because the guy who finds the deal usually gets paid. Be a deal finder, and the money will find you.]

Buying with no money down isn't commonplace, nor is it easy to do. But it's not impossible. If you care more about the monthly return than you do about getting cashed out, this strategy could be for you. It's something that you have to be on the lookout for constantly. Keep that in the forefront of your mind because opportunities do present themselves regularly, especially for those who are aware of the possibility. You have to be in the right situation where it makes sense for both parties, the seller and the buyer.

That still leaves the question, how do you do it?

Whether you deal with a seller who owns a property free and clear or the seller who has a banknote on it, there are multiple ways to buy with no money down. First, you can take over the note if there are past due payments, and you believe you can catch up on the note over time. If you take over the note, it's possible you could refinance and get cash out as well.

When you take over a deed in the right scenario, you can come away with a property investment and probably get some cash. If you take over the deed and then refinance, you will get the true ARV (After Repair Value) out of it. More than likely, the property will need work, so you'll use some or all of the refinance money for needed repairs. On the rare occasion it doesn't need any work, you'll be able to put some of that money in your pocket right away at the closing table.

CHAPTER
FIVE

How Does Owner Financing Work?

As odd as it may sound to you, owner financing is much easier than any other kind of financing. If you get a yes from the owner, the sky is pretty much the limit, including the possibility of no money upfront on a deal. Besides taking over loans on residential properties, which are "subject to" the existing mortgage, most of the owner financing deals I have done have been on large commercial properties. Before I get into the specifics of owner financing, I want to review traditional lending channels with you.

The first commercial property I bought was in 2013. It's a two-story multi-unit located in greater Las Vegas. The deal was easy to do because I was able to obtain an SBA (Small Business Administration) loan with excellent terms. When I took possession, the place was nearly empty. But the good news was that renting out just the first floor paid all my rent and expenses. At first, I used the second floor for my office, but that floor was later divided into a number of individual suites, which allowed me to refinance the property for capital growth.

Banks are far tougher than property owners when it comes to financing. Their loan representatives lack compassion; terms are not generous toward the borrower, and rules are rigid. I would pursue all loan deals that a bank rejected if I thought a denial decision was wrong because that was often the case. Banks make decisions based on the supposition the applicant will fail. They are fully aware of the failure rate from historical records, so if that building the bank is financing is not going to pay for the loan, then they are going to want enough down payment to cover their costs and also make sure they make a healthy profit if they have to "call the loan" (demand full payment of the remainder of the loan immediately). However, every single one of my plans is based on careful scrutiny and a goal to succeed. Sometimes it could take several passes at a bank or other lending institution to convince the powers that be I was worthy of the loan. Top tip: You have nothing to lose by going back to the bank if you've been turned down for a loan. Re-making your case by presenting better illustrations or scenarios makes you personally stronger going forward and builds respect for you in the eyes of the lender. Grit and determination are admirable traits, so walk in confidence and show them your best stuff.

Commercial lending in Nevada is tough. When I first went out to apply for loans, early on and often, no bank would even consider loaning me money for financing (it felt almost like they were laughing at me, which made me even more determined). The SBA loan I did get on the first commercial building purchase was primarily because my real estate business qualified for it; and also the fact that the first floor of the building would cover the loan, so it was a no-brainer for the bank. I only needed one of the offices, so after I met the obligations of the SBA, the building cash flowed nicely.

The second commercial property I bought was a multi-unit building in close proximity to the first one. I had decided to find something that was a better space for my office. Just a year after I bought the first building, I found what I call the Rainbow property in 2014. Rainbow is a 14,000 sq ft single-story office building. It was perfect for investment - mostly leased, except for two suites. The building was designed in the 1980s with a maze-like layout and rounded corners detailing the architecture. The L-shaped building was divided into two major sections or sides. At the time I was considering this purchase, one of the sections accommodated the space needs of a physician, including a reception area, clinical exam rooms, and pathology labs. The other section had been utilized most recently as a real estate sales office. In the 30 years of the building's existence at the time, its history included leases by businesses of many types because of its ideal proximity to both downtown Vegas and vital outlying communities, as well as its enormous free parking lot. I wanted to buy the building because of those features and because it was close to my other building. I knew they would work well together. As you grow on the commercial side, it's important to consider how your properties work together. If you have many office buildings, you will have many location and space selections to show your prospective clients.

I took the financing deal to Meadows bank, the same bank that did my SBA loan on the first building. Meadows is a local bank that is affiliated with retired tennis star and favorite son of Las Vegas, Andre Agassi. The building was for sale for $1,450,000. I had structured the deal with a total of $450,000 down, with the seller carrying $250,000 of that amount. So that left me with having to come up with $200,000, which at the time was a huge stretch. We brought the deal to the bank, and they nuked it. The rep said, "Give us $750,000 down, and we'll do the deal. That was not going to work, so we walked away.

As we left, the owner and I looked at each other, and he said, "We're not going to let the bank get in the way of this deal." The owner, Rex, and I had become friendly with one another. Rex was a CPA and had taught school, but he really was at the end of his investing career and ready to retire. He said to me, "We will get this deal done." Here's what we agreed: I gave him the full amount we were going to give to the bank (yes, I had to strrretchhhh even more), and he financed the balance with a real estate contract between the two of us. No appraisal, no inspection, nothing else. Just, "Here's the money down, and here's the interest." We got the deal done quickly. When the note matured (came due), we tweaked it, and I paid it off eventually through refinancing.

Here's a cool follow-up story. There's no better referral than the guy you just finished paying $1,450,000 plus interest! In 2018, when I was in the process of making the final payment to Rex, I was also out shopping for more property, and Rex put in a good word for me. I had never intended to do owner financing when I bought the property from Rex, but it was a necessity to keep the deal together between us. Actually, putting into action what I had learned and seen over the years was a bit of a scary (but totally exhilarating) time for me. We're always a bit scared at the beginning of a new adventure. Starting to invest (or do big owner financing) is like everything else - the more you do, the better you'll get.

In 2016, while visiting Miami, Florida, my car got towed, and it cost $240 to get it returned to me. I fought like hell, but in the end, the towing company still got my $240 CASH, and there was not a thing I could do about it. At the time, I had been looking for a new business venture, and after my experience in Miami, towing became a good business to consider for acquisition. It felt almost as if a towing company was the "house" when it came to parking, and in Vegas, you just don't beat the house.

Richard, a friend and fellow real estate investor, owned a tow business there with his wife. We had actually discussed partnering earlier, but it never worked out. Eventually, I would pay them $130,000 for one working truck, a license, and some junk cars. I would pay even more dearly with my time, money, energy, and stress with what would come later, but I can tell you one thing, the tow business is a great business - for finding real estate.

I made almost no money with the tow business because of all the expenses needed to build it up to a level that could develop and sustain sizable civic contracts. I lost a lot of time, made some enemies, made some friends, but also learned a few lessons. Two lessons I thought I already knew were emphasized and magnified: 1) It's not what you know, it's who you know, good or bad. 2) All politics are local.

Newer lessons learned include: Real estate is more profitable than towing; your network is your net worth; stay in your lane. All these lessons sound cliché until you come to realize the importance of them through your personal experience. I will not bore you with details of my encounters with local governing bodies that regulate the tow industry. Suffice it to say that I was incentivized to move back to the comfort of real estate investing and look at new business opportunities that support this dynamic sector of our economy, such as YouTube and social media.

Even though I didn't enjoy direct monetary success in the tow business, the real estate I found while evaluating lots for my towing business made me millions. I bought three properties while searching for the perfect lot. One of those properties is one of my favorite owner financing stories.

In 2017, I made the purchase of a 2.3-acre parcel of land on Fremont Street in Las Vegas. Several months after purchasing the parcel, I got a message from the owners of the property next door notifying me that I had an old well that was eroding their asphalt driveway. Once I had the driveway issue handled, we started talking about their property. I mentioned that if they were ever interested in selling it, to let me know. As it turned out, the owners were thinking of selling and also were open to owner financing. They wanted $1.5 million. I thought the selling price was fair, so my focus was on negotiating the down payment and the interest. We agreed on the price, but I did not agree on the 6% interest they wanted, so I knocked it down to 5%. They also asked for a 30% down payment, but I knocked that down to 20%. Clearly, in this situation, the sellers were more sophisticated and wanted more money upfront and over time. However, we finally did agree on my numbers for interest and down payment.

"My main focus when negotiating a deal with a seller is to pay the least amount of interest possible."

When I'm doing an owner-finance deal, and we're focusing on the most important thing to the seller, which is the monthly payment, I also need to keep in focus what's important to me. Paying no interest at all is the most ideal, so I will include the words "fixed payment" during the negotiation. To me, a fixed payment means "no interest"; to the seller/owner, it means "how much I am getting paid every month."

If the owner asks me what kind of interest they're getting for the fixed payment, I will lead the conversation back to "I'm giving you a fixed payment for X number of years." If the owner continues to inquire about the rate of interest, I will start that discussion with, "How's 1% for you?" The lower your interest, the better your return. If you can keep the focus on a fixed payment and low-interest rate, you will maximize your return over both the short and long terms.

Explain that you know what you're doing and that you will put everything in the terms of the contractual agreement. If the owner is willing to do it the way you set things up during negotiation, and is prepared to sign the written agreement, make sure that you are covered legally. You should have an attorney help you write the agreement or at least look it over for you. We live in a litigious society, so always make sure that you protect yourself, especially if you're a sophisticated investor. Owner financing is usually initiated by the buyer, so know what you want before going in for the ask. Keep in mind the following as you consider your options:

> "Desire is the starting point of all achievement, not a hope, not a wish, but a keen pulsating desire, which transcends everything. Weak desire brings weak results."
>
> \- *Napoleon Hill*

Owner financing could be structured as a promissory note, as a contract for deed, or at times it could also just be agreed upon between the two of you. The most important thing to remember is that the seller acts as the bank, and you are negotiating the terms, so you'll want to make sure that the terms are best for you. Let's return to the meaning of "subject to" and how it can benefit you when dealing with real estate.

Subject to, or sub to, means "conditionally upon" a thing or event. Normally, it is the existing mortgage that the deal is subject to in a real estate contract: In plain English, we're buying the house and taking legal ownership through the deed, "subject to the existing mortgage."

What does that effectively mean? It means you are entitled to be called a creative finance person now. When you buy a property from the owner on contract, sometimes it may be desirable to keep the mortgage in their name. Why would anyone do that? Here's where "subject to" can be used with creativity. Let's say you have a property that you are chasing. It has an imminent foreclosure, and you have spoken to the owner, who already has walked away from paying the mortgage. Their good credit is seemingly destroyed. You can say, "Hey there, Mr. or Ms. Seller, don't give up. If you allow me to buy the house from you subject to the existing mortgage, I can reinstate the mortgage, pay off the late payments and get some money in your pocket for working with me."

What?

OK, stay with me. When I first started, I had no hard money lenders nor enough cash to do more than one home at a time. Lenders really don't like financing fixers, so at that time, it was either hard money or cash, and again, I had neither. Therefore, I chased a lot of foreclosures that had equity (the value of a mortgaged property after deduction of charges against it) or potential equity if the property could be sold at the right price. Usually, owners who are in foreclosure have tried everything (or tried nothing); they are at the end of their rope, there is no time to list, and I might be their only option. I would buy these properties subject to the existing mortgage, reinstate the mortgage, fix the house, sell it, pay off their mortgage, and give the owner some cash. It was a big, beautiful win for everyone! I have lots of references because of how I handled myself in those cases. I always made sure it was a win for each of us. Think of the alternative: The seller loses the house and all equity and is left with the heavy weight and personal shame of a foreclosure on their credit report. The bank loses all the past payments and has to take over fixing and maintaining the property until a buyer can be found. Win-win-win or lose-lose? The answer is obvious.

The concept of subject to is not limited to just mortgages. You could buy a house subject to a judgment or lien, for example. Basically, subject to recognizes some type of encumbrance (burden or impediment) on the title to the house and purchase is made according to that recognition. I bought a house during probate (more on probate in the next chapter), and it got somewhat crazy. Another local Vegas wholesaler had it for a year and couldn't get it done. The house was upside down by all accounts, meaning that the person who originally owned it (I was trying to buy the probate property from the decedent's sister) had all sorts of liens: a mortgage lien for $166,000, a lien for $13,000 placed by the homeowners' association, and a $200,000 lien placed by UMC (University Medical Center of Southern Nevada). The owner was in UMC Hospital at the time of death. When a Medicaid patient dies at the UMC Hospital, it is UMC policy to place a medical lien on properties in order to collect unpaid medical bills (one big reason why you should have your property in a trust). I thought the hospital would probably settle for a lesser amount. When I talked to the couple (the decedent's sister and husband), they were really excited at the prospect of finally getting their money. The death had been quite a few years before, the property was just sitting there, and they were working with a second wholesaler who had also failed. They were reluctant to go through it again with me because the other guys could not get it done.

This was one of those deals where I was trying to stop the foreclosure, and I had only a few days to stop the process. So that meant lots of calls to the bank and Fedexing documents to the couple who lived out of state. They got a bit impatient because they had been waiting a year. I had told them they would get paid subject to (pun, but true) me obtaining a release of the medical lien or substantial renegotiation of the amount due to UMC. A few months went by, and we were not moving very fast on negotiating with UMC. The scenario was bleak. The lawyer for the hospital knew that the hospital would get paid only if and when I sold the probate property. If the property went all the way down to full foreclosure, the hospital could end up getting nothing since they were a junior lienholder to the mortgage company, which would get their principal, interest, and penalties first. The couple wanted to get paid, but I knew that I might not win the battle. It could be a good payoff, but it was a big gamble for me. We settled on an immediate $5,000 payment to the couple, no matter whether I won or lost (whether I got to sell the house or it was foreclosed). I am certain they needed the money more than they could wait, so they were happy. [It was a good move by the couple because it did take me another year or so to finalize a deal.] I hired an attorney to stop the sale and negotiate the UMC lien. I learned a long time ago in dealing with hospital liens to start low and stay low. We originally offered them $1,000, went up by small increments, and finally settled on $7,500. During the time that it took us to negotiate, I put a renter in the property to offset some of the legal costs. I let him know in writing that the property was in foreclosure, and I could not guarantee that the foreclosure would not happen; but that we were battling with the bank and hopeful of getting it resolved. I discounted the rent by several hundred dollars and had a happy renter. The rent almost covered all my costs, except for those needed to flip the property.

I made great money on that deal - my costs to get in were really low. I bought the house for the cost of my attorney's fees and the small bit of repair work I did to make it rent-ready. I controlled the property (rented and collected income) until I eventually sold it. I could have kept it as a rental for that little bit of money once we resolved the UMC lien issue, but I wanted the cash to buy more cheap houses. I wish I had that property, but you always do!

To summarize, don't let your conventional thinking limit you. All things are possible. The deed controls the interest to the property, but that deed's interest could be overcome by a masterlease on the property, which could be further controlled by the lease of a tenant. Real estate involves all sorts of interesting and fun things that you can learn from others. I did not invent or create anything that I am talking about; I simply watched someone else take an inventive action or have read about others doing certain creative things.

You will learn by experience that a court order basically trumps everything: Meaning, if you have title issues, and you know that you can win the battle in court, you can alter virtually everything on a title. [As you probably already know, some laws are nutty.] We bought a property in New Orleans from the administrator of an estate, where the mortgage was wiped out completely by and through the succession (Louisiana term for probate). Anything is possible! A house we still own in New Orleans was purchased subject to payment of $48,000 in back taxes. We refinanced the house with a bank, got a construction loan, and have been renting it out as a duplex ever since. Essentially, we are in that property for $0 because the value of the house appraised for a lot more than the taxes, so the bank loaned us all the money needed for renovation. It was a major job because the house had been vacant for 20 years, and the surrounding area had changed for the better. The rental has been very cash flow positive for seven years, it's probably worth $500,000, and we only owe about $300,000! Time to sell it and put the equity to work in a better investment.

Don't read this book, subject to you <u>not</u> doing the work that goes into real estate investing. All the knowledge you will gain from this book (and others) is great, but nothing teaches better than doing!

CHAPTER

SIX

How Can You Make Money in Probate?

PROBATE IS THE term for a legal process in which a will is reviewed by the court to determine whether it is valid and authentic. Probate also refers to the general administration of a deceased person's will or the estate of a deceased person without a will. When the deceased has a trust, the court generally does not need to intervene. A probate proceeding is not always required upon death but is usually essential when a deceased person's remaining estate is of high value.

After an asset-holder dies, the court appoints either an executor named in the will or an administrator (if there is no will) to administer the process of probate. This involves collecting the assets of a deceased person to pay any liabilities remaining on the person's estate and to distribute the assets of the estate to beneficiaries. [I have dealt with this process in Louisiana, where it is called succession, but it's essentially the same thing as probate.] In probate cases, there may be real estate involved, which the heirs will need help with in determining value and/or repair and sale. That is a potential investment opportunity.

So how do you find probate deals?

- Search for abandoned properties
- Search obituaries

- Search delinquent tax registers
- Search local court filings on probate

Probate, by definition, involves the death of somebody. These deals require sensitivity because you will be dealing with the loved ones of a deceased person. You may need to locate the person who was made the heir to the property, and you should think about how you would go about conducting the transaction with that person. How are you going to get this deal done? There are multiple ways to set up probate deals, and not all of them are going to benefit you, so if you're interested in this type of investing, you will need to learn the ins and outs of probate. It's very important that you research and understand the rules of probate within your particular state. I strongly suggest you interview several attorneys and explain to them exactly what you intend to do, which is to buy probate properties. From the very beginning, you need to let the chosen attorney know that you're the client, not the heir(s) of the deceased; and that the job of your attorney is to bind the assets through probate while protecting you and helping you throughout the process.

I probably have done more than 100 probate deals, but you always remember the first one, right? At the time of my first, I did not really know what probate was or how the property was transferred when someone passed. My prospective business caller Alvin had brought me a probate deal with a substantial amount of equity in it. The seller, Danny, was a sophisticated guy and the brother of the decedent. Danny was really cooperative in trying to get the deal done, and he worked with me as I struggled with the attorney I had hired specifically for this probate deal.

I'm pretty sure the attorney I had retained knew even less about the probate process than I did. As an example, she referred to the probate deal as a short sale (a short sale occurs when a homeowner in financial distress sells his or her property for less than the amount due on the mortgage). [Side note here: Just because they have the word attorney by their name does not mean they're smart or know what they're talking about.] It became obvious that I had hired an attorney who misrepresented her knowledge base. She constantly referred to the probate deal as a short sale, and I constantly questioned her use of that term to describe probate. Still, she remained stubborn about her incorrect usage while also maintaining that she was in constant communication with the bank to move the deal forward. But nothing was getting done, so I fired her.

Danny, the seller, gave me a marketing piece mailed to him by another local realtor who advertised probate experience, so I picked up the phone and called. This realtor offered to introduce me to a local attorney who was a probate expert if I agreed not to use him for listings. After the introduction, that attorney and I quickly meshed, and we put together a deal with Danny using what is called a "set aside" in Nevada probate.

In Nevada, probate rules state that you are allowed to buy property as a "set aside," for which you do not have to get court approval if the property or the equity is less than $100,000. Basically, the probate commissioner requires the submission of a number of legal documents, including an appraisal. As long as nobody objects (to the public posting), the set aside is finalized with a certificate that allows the property to be sold, along with the passing (transfer) of the title.

There are many advantageous probate rules in every state that could benefit you. However, the wrong attorney (see above) might possibly set up a probate sale incorrectly. Then, you could find yourself bidding against a property that you negotiated for previously. Fortunately, Danny did me a solid with the right attorney, and he and I went on to do 40 or so different probate deals over the next several years.

It is important that I emphasize the need to be aware of the rules before going into a probate deal because every state is different in the way proceedings are conducted. Make sure you are educated in at least the basics of the flow of those proceedings. Also, the laws and rules regarding probate in each state are under constant review and change, so you must have someone in the legal profession available to stay up with them. Good attorneys know the laws well and are often instrumental in crafting changes to them.

That brings up a story (we'll get into this more in a later chapter) about asset protection and probate/trust. When I first really got off the ground with real estate investing, I was on a buying frenzy that continues to this day. It wasn't long before I came to realize that I had a lot to lose, should a legal action of some sort result in an unfavorable outcome for me. It was time to protect myself.

I interviewed six Probate/Trust and Asset Protection attorneys in Nevada over the course of several weeks. Each state has its own laws, and in Nevada, there is a legal procedure called a "charging order." [In Nevada, a charging order is the only legal procedure that personal creditors of a Nevada Limited Liability Company (LLC) member can use to get at a member/debtor's LLC ownership interest. A charging order directs the LLC to pay to the creditor any distributions of income or profit that would otherwise be distributed to the LLC member/debtor.] When I met with each of the Nevada attorneys, the first thing they asked was, "Are you being sued, or do you have a judgment against you?" To all of them, I responded, "No, but down the road, odds are that I will be sued, and I want to be prepared and protected."

When you run a business, a lawsuit can happen, and usually for a frivolous reason, in my experience. However, setting up a trust and LLC with ASSet protection strategies will help protect your assets, and limit the amount of income tax you pay, based on what corporate tax status you choose: S Corp., C Corp., Sole Proprietorship, etc. A corporate structure is based on a legal document. If you don't understand how the structure described on that piece of paper works and/or it is not written correctly, you have garbage. You definitely need capable people working for you on legal matters. A few of the attorneys I met with were very proud of their work: The legal fees quoted ranged from $2,500 to $25,000 for the same thing. I am fortunate to have several great attorneys who represent my interests. They are just people underneath the suits, degrees, and titles, just like all the rest of us. My best advice for locating good attorneys: Look for or request referrals from your associates for smart and moral people who also are experienced attorneys (in real estate, using an inexperienced rookie for a lawyer could have disastrous consequences). Surrounding yourself with smart people has a tendency to make you smarter versus the opposite. Good attorneys offer probate and trust classes all the time, so take those (usually free) classes, then listen and learn (this is also a decent way to take the measure of an attorney). Don't believe everything you read or hear, and always triple-check legal advice to keep yourself out of hot water.

Before I end this chapter, I want to share one of the probate deals that I was involved with and how a tragedy made worse was turned into something for the better. There was a woman (we'll call her Pam), whose daughter had passed away suddenly and tragically. The daughter's boyfriend stripped the house of any worthwhile belongings and let it go into foreclosure. Even so, the property was actually still in pretty good condition. Pam's daughter had purchased it as her first home, and it was a really nice single-story residence near the Southpoint Casino in Vegas.

When I first called Pam about a meeting, she was very skeptical about allowing me to work within probate rules on her daughter's house because it signified her daughter's death, the insensitive, greedy boyfriend, and a lot of other emotionally negative things for her. I suggested that she could remember her daughter's house differently: I would put the house back in good condition, in the way she remembered it when her daughter was alive. Then, someone new could buy that nice home, which she remembered fondly. I also informed her that she could meet with the probate attorney, bring a friend and ask questions; and that she would receive money as part of the agreement. She agreed to meet with me.

As I built her trust, Pam and I decided on a dollar amount to take over the estate, and she assigned probate interest to me. That meant I could be formally assigned, or nominated, to deal with the assets of the estate, essentially the house. I would pay the attorney upfront to do all the legal work, and Pam would be paid once the house was sold. We fixed up the house as promised and sold it. I paid Pam the agreed amount, and overall, she was pleased with the outcome of a difficult personal experience. To this day, she's still one of the first people called if I need a character reference.

Death is inevitable but is also a very sensitive subject for everyone. Being compassionate, empathetic, sympathetic, and also kindly human are key qualities to bring when working within probate deals. All families are different, and generally, when you are awarded a probate deal, you are the one picking up the pieces for the family, so make sure you use velvet gloves.

You will need a good attorney to help you during probate sales. Remember that not all attorneys have your best interests in mind. Find one that understands the following things very well:

- Their client is <u>you</u>
- Understanding of process and functions of business
- Protection of you and the probate estate

When you find an expert probate attorney who knows how to conduct a probate sale, he/she will:

- Help you to understand what the statutes are and what you legally can and cannot do
- Advise you of the best way to do the deal for you as a buyer
- Structure the contract/deal for you so it flows seamlessly through title

CHAPTER

SEVEN

My FAVORITE Real Estate Investment Strategy

MY FAVORITE REAL estate investing strategy is buying homes for cash in cheap markets. You're probably familiar with this strategy from playing the board game Monopoly®. You buy cheap homes that you can rent out so you can make what used to be called mailbox money. These days, it's money that goes straight into your bank account, as long as your tenants pay their rent. When you get enough of the "green houses," you move onto the "red hotels" (aka multi-units).

Advantages of buying cheap homes:

- Allows you to think in uncomplicated terms
- Provides regular monthly passive income
- Maintains option of selling in the future
- Has minimal carrying costs, therefore…
- Supplies good positive cash flow

You can buy in other, more affordable markets when your region's supply of cheap homes is depleted.

Hurdles:

- Markets may not be local

- Finding the cash to invest might be difficult
- Scaling (getting more cash to reinvest) could be a challenge
- It's a slower way to grow in real estate investing

In 2009, markets all over the country had crashed. I was doing well selling real estate as an REO broker in Las Vegas, and at my peak, I sold 643 homes in one year. When I visited banks and other asset management companies throughout the U.S. as a part of doing business during this period, I heard fantastic stories of properties in other states selling for just one dollar! In Detroit, the Pontiac Silverdome sold for a measly $583,000 out of market. [It cost $55.7 million to build the Silverdome in 1975!] There were 200-unit apartment buildings in Detroit selling for $50,000. At that point on my journey, I was too nervous about buying anything out of state, even though I had the money to do it. I looked at lots of properties and made lots of observations, even visiting different markets several times, but never pulled the trigger on a deal. Just the thought of buying property outside Nevada or Washington made me uncomfortable, probably because I felt I would not have full control of my investments.

"Planting that seed was the best thing that happened, though, because when the opportunity presented itself again later on, I was ready to take action."

If you're somebody who's ready to start multiplying your money by investing in real estate, then you need to start:

- Acquiring massive amounts of properties in an area where you can do that at a fast pace

- Consider purchasing in a different market from where you live after your properties have appreciated and gained some equity

That doesn't necessarily mean you have to travel across the country to find deals. There are small-town markets outside of big cities, everywhere around the U.S. Go online and hunt for deals that you can drive to within a day.

Once you've acquired a property, you can utilize technologies that allow you to manage properties from afar.

- You can set up locks with key codes for showings, so you don't even have to hire a realtor
- To hire a handyman, use sites like Angie's List
- Utilize Facetime/WhatsApp to manage contractors
- Install Ring camera for security, or game camera triggered by motion (either one is a cost-effective way to see what's going on via WiFi without being there
- Install a security system or make the home smart (Wi-Fi permitting)

There are plenty of tools to help you invest in other markets. Unless you're a total control freak, there's no need for you to be there physically. Understand that if you're new to a market, you absolutely need to go there initially to check it out. Do you need to continue to go there? Only if you're a beginner. It's a good idea to go back several times after you purchase a property in a new market to get a fuller understanding of the area.

If you're buying a large number of properties, then you'll need some representation by a local agent or lawyer. If you're an experienced investor, then you'll definitely want to have somebody there on the ground looking after your interests. Hire a property manager that you know and trust, and work to build up that relationship as part of your growing business.

One of the keys to my investing success in other markets out of state is acquiring great property managers. I have a property manager in Mississippi named Alain, who has become a good friend. Alain manages most of my rentals there, and we have grown together. Alain and I first met in 2011, when I was trying out buying investment property in an inexpensive market. I have liked Mississippi since I was a kid (actually thought seriously about going to college at Ole Miss) and thought property there would be a good value based on prevailing laws, cash flow, and long-term growth. You can see which way a city is going by the infrastructure and the movement, especially if you're an outsider or don't go there very often. Biloxi, Mississippi is up and coming and has provided great investment opportunities for me in the rentals market, but I have also flipped at least 40 homes over the years. Alain is now flipping, he's got some rentals, and he's changed his life for the better because of those moves. If he just continued to manage properties, he'd still have a business. But if he didn't buy houses, he would not be taking advantage of his infrastructure of management tools and vendors. Again, it's about the company you keep. He has looked after my properties as if they are his own, and because of that, we pay him right. I know a lot of guys who focus on beating down the property manager over their compensation percentages. I believe in rewards, incentives, and consequences. Why punish someone who does a good job? Why not reward them? The point is this: Make sure you have someone who can look after your interests when you invest out of state, and ideally, it should be an experienced, honest property manager who treats you and your property right. It may cost a little more than market price to get the right one, but you will have extra peace of mind, and that is priceless.

Maybe you're still wondering, how do you find a market to invest in? We'll go over that in the next chapter.

CHAPTER
EIGHT

How to Find the Right Market for Investing

BEFORE YOU FIND a market you want to invest in, analyze your risk tolerance. Things to consider:

- What's your current income?
- How much loss are you willing to take?
- Do you have a history of making bad decisions?
- What's your credit report look like? FICO score?
- Get someone else's professional opinion research first, then jump in - but don't get stuck in a market that doesn't pan out.

Let me elaborate. When I first invested in Tacoma, Washington, I had a good reason to invest in that market because my business partner John lived there. I was from ultra-high priced Issaquah, Washington, so the Tacoma area was a great value. We picked up houses for around $50-100,000 with minor and major repairs. The main point is that the houses were cheap, and I had someone (John) to look after them when I wasn't around. When I first went to Biloxi, I was actually going to try to find a piece of land for myself (I ended up buying one in Tylertown). I saw this cool little town with a great name that reminded me of a small Las Vegas on the Gulf Coast of Mississippi. Biloxi had potential. Prices were cheap, and the first house I bought was only $32,000. I bought that house from Alain, the realtor and good friend who now manages all my properties down there, ten years and hundreds of transactions after we first met. When I first went there, it was a risk. So how did I make the decision to go? To start, the $32,000 house was going to rent for $800 per month. Eviction laws were favorable to landlords; taxes were a bit high, insurance was a bit high, but overall I had a good return on investment (ROI). The first one worked, so why not try two, then three, then...now we own more than 100 total units in Mississippi. I started with one, and you can see how that goes when you do your research and due diligence. Ease in, and then perfect your steps. Once you learn the market and are comfortable with it, find the good deals and buy them. Don't try to eat like a pig, where "there are no bad deals," be more like a stealthy lion, waiting for the right opportunity to pounce on it. That's called knowing the market and what a good deal looks like. I was buying properties in Mississippi for $20,000 and less, and some for $50,000 plus, but now all those properties have appreciated considerably, especially during the COVID-19 pandemic. Many have blown up to the mid-$100,000s, with many years of cash flow behind them, if I decided to cash in. As my risk tolerance grew there, I did the math on the insurance and ditched everything but liability insurance. That move has saved me more than $100,000 per year. How many houses would have to be severely damaged for that to pencil out to my disadvantage? I did have storm damage a couple of years ago that cost me about $50,000 in roofs, but I paid cash for the repairs. Over six years of saving netted me about $600,000, so $50,000 paid out for a storm in the same time frame is not bad. Plus, I didn't have to deal with insurance companies, who famously hate paying claims.

Spend time analyzing the market you have an interest in. What do you like about it, what do you think is coming there in the foreseeable future? Then check for supporting data online. Don't rely solely on online data, but it's one good thing to check. I believe that walking and driving around while viewing a city can give you a pretty good feel. I now know that Tylertown, where I bought a piece of land, is not growing. The population of the county is 17,000 and has been going down for years. Who's going to buy my property(ies) when I want to sell them? About that land I bought...it's for sale...crickets...I repeat: Don't get stuck in a market that doesn't pan out.

- Don't speculate - only buy properties that have immediate cash flow or value
- Don't buy land unless you can rent it out immediately

"Find the closest market that you can drive to from your home."

Ideally, that market would be in your backyard (nearby), but if it's not, that's okay too. Just starting out is going to help you to become an investor faster. Sometimes, investing in your backyard first isn't going to be possible. For example, if you live in San Francisco and can't invest $2 million in a house, then you need to invest in a buy and hold strategy in a market that's less expensive. Get a map, draw a circle that represents about a 30-mile radius around where you live, and start investigating smaller markets outside your area. Start looking at the large and small markets and the sub-markets of the large markets to familiarize yourself with what's happening in those sectors of the real estate market.

"To find a market in which you can make money, you have to find one that's a certain size and fits into your budget according to your risk tolerance."

Let's say you want to invest in Seattle, Washington, but it's out of your budget. If you draw a big circle representing a 30-mile radius around the city, then you'll find Tacoma, which is a lot cheaper. That might be somewhere you can start. If you notice that Tacoma is still too expensive, you could search even further out and find Olympia. Continue to do that until you find your sweet spot.

"In high-growth areas, properties generally appreciate over the long term."

If you are in the 'rust belt' or Midwest, you're lucky because you have cheap properties all around you. A generally reliable rule of thumb is as you get outside the big cities, cheaper properties become more abundant. You can even look for even less expensive properties in other states through tax sales, but that is a strategy of patience, yet one that could pay off in big profit when you find the right deal. When you are able to wager back taxes to buy a foreclosed property at a tax auction, it's usually a pretty sweet deal. There is another way to invest in tax liens without taking actual possession of the property.

A tax lien is a legal claim against the property of an individual or business that fails to pay taxes owed to a governing body. When a property owner fails to pay the taxes on their property, the municipality or county in which the property is located has the authority to place a lien on that property. The lien acts as a legal claim against the property for the unpaid tax amount owed. That property cannot be sold or refinanced until the taxes are paid, and the lien is removed.

Investors interested in tax lien investing opportunities should contact the local tax revenue official (usually the county assessor) in the county or municipality responsible for property tax collection. Not all states provide for public sale of delinquent property tax bills, but there are currently 2,500 jurisdictions, cities, townships, or counties in the United States that sell public tax debt. If the state does allow public auction of the unpaid property tax bill, investors should be able to determine when and where these taxes are published for public review. Property tax sales are required to be advertised before the sale. Advertisements list the owner of the property, legal description, and amount of delinquent taxes to be sold.

Investors who purchase property tax liens are usually required to pay back the full amount of the lien to the issuing municipality immediately upon purchase. The tax lien issuer collects the principal, interest, and any penalties. When the tax lien is sold, the buyer/investor pays the lien certificate holder (governing body) and collects the lien certificate. The property owner must repay the investor the entire amount of the lien plus interest, which varies from one state to another - typically between 10% and 18% (consult your local municipality). If the investor paid a premium for the lien, this may be added to the amount that is repaid in some instances.

The repayment schedule usually lasts anywhere from six months to three years. In most cases, the owner pays the lien in full. If the owner cannot pay the lien by the deadline, the investor has the authority to foreclose on the property just as the municipality would have, although this happens very rarely. As with anything, you must be careful with tax lien investments.

I bought 20 tax liens in Rochester, New York, through an investment club that was hosting a tax seminar there. The instructors from the investment club who taught the class were very knowledgeable, so a group of us attending the seminar decided to invest with them. The person conducting the tax lien sales on behalf of the club was an established wholesaler of tax liens from whom we had previously purchased a few tax liens. He told me that working with this particular investment club's two managers to arrange for the tax sales was the most painful deal he had ever done. He said they were novices who fought over everything. Unfortunately, that was a sign of things to come. About $27,000 of our money didn't get placed onto tax lien purchases and was not returned by the club managers. I emailed several of the other students in the class about our experience, but at the time, they chose not to join with us in pursuing our investment funds. A year later, they contacted me with the same issues I had, asking for my help.

In order to get our money back, I had to build a website to reveal the club's unprofessional (verging on criminal) behavior. This action put a lot of pressure on the club managers. We finally got our money. When people steal from you, building a website to reveal the facts with freedom of speech is a good way to put pressure on bad actors. The two guys who ran the club dissolved their partnership, and I am sure they will have some more negative consequences from this episode. It was insane that they tried to take money from very experienced investors. Some guys are just bad with money and try to cover up their mistakes with lies. We are lucky that we got out early but are still dealing with the tax liens. You always take a risk when you invest with someone you don't know well. Sometimes people steal your money, so be careful because it can happen, even to experienced investors. [All that being said, one of the reasons I love investing in Mississippi is the availability of tax liens, and I will continue to invest in them as part of our effort there.] Investing requires a lot of research and time but has huge payouts if you are a patient person who can do research. That's enough about tax liens - let's get back to rentals.

One way to determine property appetite in a certain area is to place a "coming soon" rental ad online (without using an exact address because you don't want to get in trouble with an owner). If you put a property out there and your phone doesn't ring once, then you may want to reconsider investing in that area.

Things to do before buying rentals:

- Check out the area
- Check out the online response
- Look at the laws regarding eviction
- Research how favorable the state is to landlords
- Research the tax structure
- Calculate insurance costs
- Interview Property Managers and Realtors about the area
- Decide if you can self-manage or if you need to hire a Property Manager

How small can the market be for real estate investing? That depends. For me, small markets are too slow and take too long to get properties rented. Metropolitan Biloxi at about 68 sq miles is about as small as I'm willing to go.

If I'm looking into investing in an area like Biloxi, then I consider the fact that there are frequent hurricanes in that region. Do I need to buy insurance? As long as I'm not buying in areas that got blown away in the last hurricane, then no. I would choose to buy properties that I might lose a roof on. That's a determination I would make, according to my risk tolerance. Some people may not be comfortable with that, rather they would want the insurance. However, the extra insurance means that their return is going to go down. Your overall calculation needs to factor in the potential loss and your risk tolerance, just in case there is a hurricane.

What to look for in a larger city before investing:

- Do research on up-and-coming cities
- Check the signs of growth
- Is the city investing in itself? Rebuilding its transportation?
- Are other investors investing?
- Are investors renovating properties?
- Or are there dumpsters everywhere?

Ideally, you should find a location that is on the cusp of a great growth spurt. Get in low, stay for a while and sell high.

CHAPTER

NINE

Why You Should Invest in Multi-Units

IN 2009, A few years after moving to Las Vegas, I bought my first multi-unit. I noticed most of the smaller multi-units in Vegas are in areas that are less desirable, and that goes for other cities too. Don't let that deter you from a great opportunity! Around the greater metropolitan Seattle region where I am from, there are many good areas for multi-family investment. In places like San Diego, where you are close to the beach, you can do really well with multi-family. Inner-city multi-family can be rough, but it's possible. Perform your due diligence with area research and math models to make sure an investment is going to work first on paper, at the very least.

> **"Multi-unit properties can be as little as two units or as many as you can imagine."**

Growing wealth is all about economies of scale. Being able to use leverage with a small amount of cash down to control a large portion of real estate is why people like to buy multi-units. When you invest in multi-units, you get multiple-income properties in one general location, meaning more tenants and more money.

If you're interested in investing in multi-units, you should know that there is a major tax advantage for investors: cost segregation. A cost segregation study (studies range in price) identifies and reclassifies personal property assets to shorten the depreciation time for taxation purposes, which reduces current income tax obligations.

Personal property assets include a building's non-structural elements, exterior land improvements, and indirect construction costs. Through depreciation combined with a cost segregation study, you can accelerate your depreciation and take it as a loss on your income statement. [Make sure you consult with your CPA.]

Having your money invested in a multi-unit also can be a huge advantage for a future sales price. You are able to build up your wealth quickly because you're using a relatively small amount of money to manage a large property. If you buy one property with four units, you'll have four different tenants and four separate income streams. Along with those positives, there are some pitfalls that you need to be aware of, too, such as the fact that there are more maintenance and possibly more tenant issues with multi-units. All things considered, multi-units are going to be easier for intermediate investors to manage but can be for beginners, too.

Windsor Manor, built in1924, is a 4-story multi-unit property in Kansas City, MO that I purchased for renovation and eventual leasing. It qualifies for historic building tax credits to assist with the cost of rehab. There are many such programs available to real estate investors. [Hopefully, I will get the tax credits.]

The most important thing to remember about multi-family is that most properties are trading on "cap rates." Capitalization rates, also known as cap rates, are measures used to estimate and compare the rates of return on multiple commercial real estate properties. Cap rates are calculated by dividing the property's net operating income (NOI) by its property asset value. Cap rates determine value, and the lower the cap rate, the higher the value of the property. Commercial properties also sell based on NOI. The higher the net operating income and the lower the cap rate, the more your property will be worth. I'll give you an example because I know it's confusing and complicated, especially if you are new. So let's keep it simple. Your profit, aka NOI, has a direct line to the value (market price) of the property (what it will sell for). Once you know your cap rate, you can find ways to reduce your expenses that will increase the value of your property.

Market Value = Net Operating Income ÷ Cap Rate

Let's say the NOI is $25,000 on your eight plex. The cap rate is 10% because it's in an OK area. Generally speaking, the higher the cap rate, the worse the area.

$25,000 ÷ .10 = $250,000 market value

If that cap rate were 5%, and you did the math:

$25,000 ÷ .05 = $500,000 market value

Let's expand a little bit to show the impact of the cap rate's relationship to the NOI. Start with the lower example above of the 5% cap rate with our NOI at $25,000 for our eight plex. You just finished reading my book and decided that you are going to increase your NOI. So you meter the water for your multi-family, an expense that you had been paying for all tenants, and begin to separately bill each tenant for water consumption. This move eliminates water as an expense and creates an income stream for you instead. Now the eight plex property brings in $31,000 in NOI and totally changes the resulting equation in your favor:

$31,000 ÷ .05 = $620,000 market value!

Giving something such as water away for free has no value, so don't do it. You have seen the power of cap rates on commercial real estate. Simply increasing the annual net operating income by $6,000 increased the market value of the property by $120,000. That's why you need to completely understand how cap rates work when you invest in commercial real estate, including multi-family properties. You have a great deal of control over your destiny when investing in real estate. Use your power wisely for the best return.

CHAPTER

TEN

How You Can Retire Relatively Quickly

THE NUMBER ONE way for a real estate investor to retire relatively quickly is to buy low-cost single-family homes and hold them. When I go into a new property, I have a long-term outlook of holding for ten years, not selling. This means I will turn it into a rental property to earn passive income. If and when I sell, I will do a 1031 exchange with the proceeds from that property. I'll explain 1031s more in a later chapter.

I have used the above rule of thumb in smaller market areas. In 2011, Biloxi was the first market I invested in outside Nevada and Washington. The houses that I bought in Biloxi ranged anywhere from $8,000 to $50,000. Most of the homes had three bedrooms, at least one bathroom, and anywhere from 1,100-2,000 square feet. They were rambler ranch-style homes built in the 1950s, 60s, or 70s, and perfect for rentals. I paid cash for them, and sometimes I'd need to put a little more money into them. However, there were many examples of homes I bought for around $18,000 and would only need to put $5,000 into them to make them ready for tenants. Many of them rented out for $700, $800, $900, or $1,000 a month. My aim for each house was to net $500 at the end of the month or a $6,000 annualized return per house.

Here's how to calculate how long it would take for you to get all your cash back:

$18,000 Purchase price
+ $5,000 Renovations
= $23,000 Total Investment ÷ $6,000 year revenue
= 3 years 10 months to recover the original investment

In the example above, the purchase price is $18,000 with $5,000 worth of work for a total investment of $23,000. Divide that total by the annualized return of $6,000 ($500/month), and it would take just under 4 years to return your investment to you.

There will be times when your return on a specific property has doubled, tripled, or quadrupled very quickly. If you have another place to put the capital and make a better return on your money, then you will want to switch up your long-term plan for the better return. Generally speaking, though, going in with a 10-year hold plan will keep you on target for what you're hoping to achieve.

Let's say the goal is to put about $500 a month in your pocket by investing in lower-end houses that will rent out for area market price. If you consider how much you need to make per month in order to retire wealthy, whether it's $5,000, $10,000, or $15,000+, you can determine how many smaller properties you need to buy in order to do that. For example, let's say you have $5,000 per month in net expenses, then you could assume that you need to get ten properties in order to cover that.

10 homes × $500/month = $5,000/month

In this scenario, ownership of anything after ten properties is the mark where you start building wealth, so at 11, you'll be making $500 more per month, and at 12, you'll be making $1,000 extra per month. This is when the snowball effect of creating and building wealth really takes off. However, you should be very aware that the effect also creates a forcefield for mistakes. Don't let the excitement of wealth-building dull your sensibility. You have to be smart at all times, particularly when you experience greater growth.

Owning all these rental houses paid for in cash will make you more comfortable with your exit strategy; you have the ability to sell them anytime. It's possible to have some years that aren't very productive, but overall, you'll look at the end result as a really good return on investment long-term. Plus, if you do get appreciation, your investment could have a huge upside.

There were properties I bought in Las Vegas for $15,000 that I sold for $150,000 ten years later! However, that's an exception and not a rule. Many properties I waited longer to sell, but they were still putting money into my account each month. That's because I always have a long-term hold philosophy on everything that I touch.

> "Our only limitations are the ones we set up in our own minds."
>
> \- *Napoleon Hill*

CHAPTER

ELEVEN

How Do You Find a House to Flip?

MOST PEOPLE ARE aware of what it means to flip a house from watching reality TV shows like "Flip This House," "Flip or Flop," "Fixer Upper," the list goes on. There are even a lot of people on YouTube who are flipping, so it's not that complicated, but that doesn't make it easy.

> **"Flipping a house simply means that you're purchasing a property with the intention of fixing it up to some degree and selling it fairly quickly to make a profit."**

To start, you have to decide the price at which you're comfortable buying. I've flipped in areas where an average home costs $30,000, and I've flipped in areas with homes over a million dollars average. Where's your sweet spot? It just depends on what type of deal you're doing. Ideally, you want to identify areas in which there are lots of first-time home buyers and not many renters. This will generally be the lowest cost to enter into the market because you're targeting first-time home buyers. Do some research on how the property was purchased. You want to keep an eye out for properties that closed with loans, especially FHA loans, and VA loans.

Top Tip: You need to be able to get on YouTube, go to Home Depot, talk to people, figure it out, and get it done. That is the attitude you must have in order to flip houses. There are a lot of people who get burned when they flip because they aren't willing to do that.

"If, for whatever reason, you run out of money and the only thing you've got is a paintbrush and time, you need to be able to finish the project yourself."

The process of doing it yourself is going to teach you what it takes to flip a house. That doesn't mean you have to do it all yourself, but you have to know that you are capable of doing it yourself if need be. If you already have the skillset to do it yourself and it's easy for you, then doing your first flip yourself is a no-brainer! It's vital to your investment success to gain basic knowledge in all the areas involved in flipping and how they affect the bottom line. Tackling parts of a project on your own is a good way to learn whether your bids from contractors are in the ballpark.

How do you find a cosmetic fixer-upper?

Your first task is to search for deals in an area that's in high demand, where you know the properties sell fast, primarily to first-time homebuyers.

Prepare to invest at the average first-time homebuyer price in your area. You can determine this price by looking up the average cost of homes in your city, asking realtors about market values, and talking to many different agents to get an idea of the area prices. It doesn't hurt to get to know players in the local real estate establishments, either. You never know when you might want to partner with somebody down the line. When I started flipping actively in Las Vegas, it was very easy to understand that the subdivisions with low (aka fast) DOM (Days on Market) and an average home price were the ones I went after. But there are other things to be aware of, as well. I remember a house I bought about six years ago. The DOM was great, and investors were flipping, making lots of money.

But, I had the biggest house on the block, and it wasn't just bigger by a little; it was about 1,000 sq ft bigger than the highest square footage comparable (comp) house. Usually, that means you're going to lose a bit of money on the price per square foot. I ended up selling that house for an $8,000 loss because no one could afford it in that neighborhood. I had calculated for the loss and knew there was a risk, but I didn't realize that the extra 1,000 sqft had no value for me, but it still cost me money to rehab. Funny thing, it was also a probate deal where I had a family member that was holding out, I couldn't get him to sign, and we were planning on just placing his money with the court through an attorney; thankfully, a realtor friend named Jason got the signed contract. I paid him $10,000 to get it signed, which he happily accepted. He had offered to partner on the deal too, but I thought I had a huge payday coming. After all was said and done, he got the better end of that deal. You learn so much from your mistakes. I am always cautious now when I deal with huge homes in areas where the comps are all smaller. In Vegas and many other markets, price has a direct correlation to price per sq ft (PPSQFT). If you are selling a property for $200 a foot, but the neighborhood is topped out at a certain price below that, you can get burned, regardless of how big the home is. Make sure you factor all that in! The reverse is also true. In an area where the average PPSQFT is $200, you might get more per square foot on a smaller home because that's still the least expensive home in the market just because it's the smallest, so you might be able to sell those homes for more per square foot, maybe $210 or $220. You have to evaluate everything carefully when calculating value.

You also need to determine how much money it's going to cost to repair whatever you purchase. There are tools online you can use to get a better idea of how to calculate that accurately. Smart investors calculate the before value and the after value of the house, commonly referred to as the after repair value, or ARV. The true before value is key: Maybe the house is overpriced, and that's causing a high number of days on market. Before you make an offer, run your own set of current comps in the immediate area to see what is really what. This is simple to do; you can go on Zillow or to the public tax records, see the homes that have sold in the last 6 months in the subdivision, then go out from there. Make sure you talk to a realtor, too!

Ideally, you want to be a discount home buyer, so there will almost always be repair costs involved. If you're buying a cosmetic fixer and your projected ARV is $100,000, but it needs $10,000 worth of repairs, then you want to stay at about $55,000 when purchasing. The general rule to calculate the purchase price is to take 65% of the ARV minus repairs, as shown below.

$65,000 = 65% of projected ARV ($100,000) – $10,000 repairs = $55,000 purchase price

To be a good investor, especially starting out, you want to stay close to that 65% number to calculate purchase price in order to sustain long-term profitable growth. Generally, the quicker you can fix a house, the more you can pay for the house. Let's say I was thinking about buying the above house in Vegas for $55k because it was worth $100k and needed $10k in repairs: (65% of $100k = $65k – $10k repairs = $55k). But, I think I could get the repairs finished in two weeks, because the houses generally are not that old, so repairs are easier. Then, I would be able to list and sell the house fast because inventory in Vegas moves quickly. In that scenario, I might pay 75% ARV (75% of $100k = $75k – $10k repairs is $65k purchase price) for that house because I can turn it (sell it) and get my money quickly. On the other hand, if you buy a house valued at $100k in New Orleans, most likely it was built in the 1880s out of barge board and needs $30,000 in repairs that will take three months to complete. You will want to pay close attention to holding the line at 65% ARV and being accurate about the cost of repairs. At the present time, the price of lumber in the COVID-19 era is way up and creates a negative impact on the cost of reframing a house wherever you are! Also make sure you factor in your cost of money (interest), insurance and applicable taxes, which are referred to in real estate transactions as closing costs.

CHAPTER

TWELVE

How Do You Build Credit and Get Financing?

MY FAVORITE REAL estate investment strategy requires the ability to get good financing, so you've got to have good personal and business credit. This is a principle that I learned later in life after watching people with better financing ability surpass my gains more quickly. There are multiple ways to get good personal credit. To keep my credit in good standing, I like to use credit monitoring apps like Credit Karma, which allow me to monitor my credit for free. There are other tools available to help you, but make sure you know your credit score and keep a steady eye on it.

Lenders require a minimum FICO score of 620 or more for a borrower to be qualified for a loan on an investment property; ideally, it should be at least 660 for people to take you seriously. You'll get the best breaks on interest rates at 720 and above. If you're planning to hold a property long-term, then having a higher credit score will help you get a lower percentage rate. With flipping, it won't matter as much.

Consumer financing is the hardest to get, which is one great reason why you want to work to become an investor and obtain commercial financing. Commercial financing is easier to get because a lender knows that when a property is cash flowing positively, there's less risk for them. There's been a lot of emphasis on having perfect credit, but it's not that important when you're starting out. It's better just to get started and work on repairing it as you go.

Whether you have $50,000 or little money in the bank, you will want to have a lot of credit at your disposal to grow your business. Obtaining access to credit is key for lender financing of your projects. For example, when you have good credit but you're short on cash, you can use interest-free balance transfers that will allow you to float out payment of repairs costs for months until you sell the house. However, zero interest offers are made available only to people who have good credit histories. Having a good or excellent credit score is the cornerstone of building your credit reliability so that you qualify for programs such as balance transfers.

How do you get good credit?

One of the major components of how your credit score is calculated is your debt-to-income ratio. If you have $50,000 in the bank, but you're only carrying $1,000 in credit, you've got a low credit card utilization ratio. You may have a lot of cash on hand, but you aren't utilizing enough credit to raise your FICO score. In order to do that, you need to ask for increases in the balances of any credit cards you already have and also ask for increases for your credit lines. That's just one way to raise your score.

Another thing to keep in mind is that your revolving debt can help you. This debt is the balance you have from any revolving credit, the most well-known type being credit cards. A home equity line of credit is in the same category. You might be wondering, how can having debt help? By keeping your credit utilization low and making your payments on time, that's how! (Non-revolving debt comes from installment loans like car loans, student loans, and personal loans.) Credit is super complicated, but the rule of thumb is, pay your bills on time, don't have collections or lates (late payments), and keep your balance low and your limit high. Follow that formula, and you'll be good.

One way to guarantee that you keep your score low is by applying for needless applications. Don't do that. Only apply for good credit. If you can live without it, don't buy a new car. Get a credit card, make your necessary purchases on it, and pay it off every month. That's the best way to establish credit quickly. If you need to get financing on something big, you can utilize it, but don't use it for anything else if you can use a credit card instead. If you're looking to start repairing your credit, there are many companies you can utilize, but Lexington Law is one I have used, know and trust.

How does a credit score affect your ability to get funding? Banks lend money to people who have good credit and pay their bills. There is relationship banking, but that's on the commercial side. Your credit score doesn't matter really as much unless, of course, you're a deadbeat; the lender will see that, and it will matter. But if you have a good lender and a mortgage late payment popped up and knocked your credit down 250 points because the bank made an error (happened to me), no one cares about helping you in the consumer financing world until you fix the late payment, even if it's not your fault. That is why I borrowed $600,000 from my apartment complex in Mississippi to fund my new home construction build in Kansas City; because I got denied on my loan. The same lender who denied me a loan to build my house because of the mortgage late, loaned me $2,500,000 for an apartment building I had just bought in Kansas City. And that same lender loaned me some money on some rentals I have. But on my personal house, he told me, "Sorry Troy,

I can't lend you money to build your house. Consumer Financing is hyper-regulated, and that late mortgage payment regardless of how many properties you own, or who you are, means no thanks!" I know banks can be finicky, so I always have a workaround when I get a denial. You just have to find another way. Once I finish building my home, I'll just refinance it and pull the cash out since the late payment is now off my credit report.

I hate dealing with consumer financing. The requirements put in place as a result of the passage of the Dodd-Frank bill are ridiculous. These days, every time I deal with a mortgage broker, it feels like I just got a physical exam head to toe, including ear, nose, and throat. Applications for loans become an audit of all your assets. Having a banker that you can call and say, "Hey, I've got this property over here, and I am going to buy it, because it cash flows and has a debt coverage ratio of X." That's bank speak for "The investment pays for the cost of the loan or debt service."

We are in a credit-driven society, and understanding credit and debt is key to succeeding in real estate. It also affects how properties are sold. Some properties are not financeable, and in that situation, you find out how much credit matters. [Think about why student loans are so expensive: If the costs of college education were based on cash payments, there would be a lot fewer students and revenue, but because the government backs student loans, those costs are going up stratospherically higher!]

One of the main reasons I have good credit is because when I was a young man, my Dad told me I would need credit. He said, "You need to establish credit, so start out small and easy with a JC Penney card." And that's what I did; my initial credit limit was

$100. I would buy things and pay the card balance on time every month. Then I got a Bank of America card, maxed it out in college at $2,000, but I still made my payments on time every month. Now I have cards with no limits on them. They sure help in business, not to mention the great perks that I receive, such as free air travel for my entire family!

Southwest Airlines is my favorite credit card that I use for for all business expenses. [If you're going to be charging any money for your flips or other property investments, I recommend you go to https://www.referyourchase1card.com/226/52Q1V3M02G. Then, sign up and get 50,000 free rewards points, which are worth some flights and a companion pass.] The airline and its card are fantastic, and until I get my jet, I will always fly Southwest, if they are going to my destination.

Having credit is great, credit has rewards, and it's necessary to have good credit to grow your business. But don't use credit on stuff you don't need, or that doesn't make you money. Use credit to get to where you want to be, not in the hole.

Here are some Top Tips to take care of your credit and credit report:

- Monitor your FICO score. Utilize a website like Credit Karma. Knowing your starting point will help you make a plan. Keeping track of your score will help you understand the level of borrowing for which you can get approved.

- Apply for credit only when needed. Too many inquiries will lower your score. Make sure you use credit cards only when necessary.

- Revolving credit. Some debt is "good" debt:
    - Credit cards
    - Home equity line of credit
- How to build credit effectively with good debt
    - Make payments on time
    - Keep credit utilization low
- Debt to balance ratio
    - On your credit cards:
        - Keep your balances low (use 25% or less of the limit).
        - Pay off balances each month if you can.
        - Don't spend more than 25% of the total balance on one card.

Meeting with the construction crew at the site of our new home, which Eden and I are building in Kansas City, MO.

CHAPTER
THIRTEEN

Why You Need to Have Exit Strategies

WHAT ARE YOU going to do if your first plan doesn't work out? From the start, you need to have plan A, plan B, plan C, plan D, and so on. The more exit strategies you have for a property, the more attractive it is because you have clear paths to take if your original plan doesn't work. It's important to be able to evaluate when something isn't working as planned, so you can change your plan of action; otherwise, you could go broke.

For example: When your first strategy is to flip a property, and you list it, but it goes a month without selling, you reduce the price. If it still doesn't sell, and you continue to do that month after month, it becomes a drain on your finances. At some point, you need to turn it into a rental property, which is a long-term hold. Prior to buying that property, you would have to do the math to make sure that as a rental property, it's going to cash flow what you need, so you don't go further into the hole.

Consider more possible outcomes if your initial plan doesn't work out: Could it become an Airbnb if your city allows those? You've just renovated this property; can you now rent it out for a higher return than a long-term rental? Can you sell it as owner financing and possibly sell it for a smaller down payment and a larger payment per month to get out of the deal? Can you make a contract for deed/bond or deed?

The last thing you want to do is let the property go into foreclosure. You don't want to damage your credit. It will be important when you become a more sophisticated investor and you're looking to borrow from banks. They want to make sure you meet your obligations and that you pay back your debt.

Some of my best flips were properties that didn't sell initially. If that happened, I would put in a renter, fix all the issues, rent for a year or so, and then put the property on the market. There were times I made even more money doing this! Be patient; time is on your side as long as you are making good decisions.

I started working hard at a young age. Here I am at four, clearing rocks from one of our gardens in the backyard. Struggle makes you stronger.

CHAPTER

FOURTEEN

Why You Need a Smart Accountant

IN 2008, I was just starting to get going as a real estate agent, and I got audited. Being the rookie I was, I had failed to notify the IRS of some of the previous year's income, probably because I misplaced a 1099 or some other form. The IRS informed me that I owed $8,000 in taxes.

I hired an accountant to conduct the audit, and I noticed that things kept going sideways. She'd tell me conflicting information, then provide me with more paperwork. At some point, I realized that she didn't know what she was doing, so I went without her to introduce myself to the IRS auditor. He explained to me what had been happening. Every time he asked her for some information, the accountant would provide him with something other than for what was asked and make excuses for her dereliction. This led the auditor to believe that the issue was unreported income. I tried to explain why I thought I didn't have to pay, but it didn't matter. In the end, I had to write an $8,000 check to the IRS. That's how I learned the importance of having a good CPA who understands real estate.

"A smart accountant can and will save you thousands of dollars."

After that experience with the IRS, each time I interviewed a new CPA, the first thing I did was describe the above situation. Then I'd ask, "How would you make sure this never happens to me again?"

When I asked CPA Mark Sherman this question, he answered, "I would go to the IRS website and check what income people have reported against your SSN before I file the taxes, so an audit isn't triggered." Once I had him on my team, he taught me all kinds of tax strategies to defer taxes indefinitely and other legal ways to avoid different taxes. Make sure you find an accountant who understands real estate thoroughly. If you find one early on in your investing career, you will be glad you did. Not only will they save you money, but they'll also save you time and headaches too.

I know taxes are boring, but they affect your bottom line in a big way. The more you get into commercial real estate and start to become a sophisticated investor, understanding of taxes and tax loopholes is going to help make you wealthier. Once you understand accounting, you'll realize it's more about how you do your paperwork and prepare your tax form presentations to the IRS versus anything else.

I have a hard head sometimes. When I first decided to sell some properties and put the profit into another property, I was overwhelmed with the idea of 1031 exchanges. I thought, "What's that? Nah, too complicated, just sell them and pay the tax." When my accountant discovered what I was doing, he took the time to remind me of the value of a 1031 exchange.

In brief, a 1031 exchange is the best tool in your real estate investing toolbox, sitting right next to cost segregation. A 1031 exchange allows you to take an investment property that you have had a gain on and defer the tax. Here's an easy example: Let's say I bought a house in Vegas a while back for $15,000. It's now worth $150,000. If I simply sell it, my capital gain is $135,000, and I would be taxed on that gain with a significant capital gains tax, which ranges as high as almost 40%! Just selling it means I would have to write a big check to the IRS. However, if I use a 1031 exchange, I pay no tax! All I have to do is buy a property that costs at least one dollar more than what I sold my property for, and I pay no taxes. What if you need some of that cash? How do you get access to it? Do a refinance: that's tax-free money, regardless of whether you do a 1031 exchange. [I will elaborate more on 1031 exchanges in Chapter Sixteen.]

My accountant's education and advice on 1031s is the most profitable tax counseling I have ever received. A good CPA is worth their weight in gold. They view and think about things differently than the rest of us do. If you can learn even a small part of how they think, you will be able to see opportunities through their eyes. Accounting is all about paperwork and presentation and understanding the tax code. The Federal Tax Code is long because it's set up for deductions. Most accountants aren't excited about their profession, and most don't teach you. Try to find someone who will teach you how to invest wisely and take the most legal deductions. Hire a good accountant, and make sure you go to seminars to learn from other great accountants. One of my favorite books is "Rich Dad, Poor Dad," by Robert Kiyosaki, who made a fortune in real estate investing (Kiyosaki now owns about 8,000 properties). CPA and author Tom Wheelwright is his tax advisor and has co-authored with him. Tom is a genius, and he does seminars, so I encourage you to attend one as soon as feasible. [I am really lucky to have a photo taken of Tom and me at a seminar several years ago.]

How did I go from getting audited for my taxes and paying hundreds of thousands of dollars in taxes to loving my tax returns? Because I now know the power of 1031 exchanges and cost segregation? I owe it all to my accountant, CPA Mark Sherman, who I thank regularly.

[What exactly is Cost Segregation? It's pretty complicated, so check out my YouTube Channel for the video on Cost Segregation or the Podcast that will be out by the time you read this. Make sure you like, follow and share with a friend. You'll thank me!]

CHAPTER

FIFTEEN

How Important Is Bookkeeping?

BOOKKEEPING IS EXTREMELY important and is not something you can do easily as an afterthought. You need to stay in front of this process because if you get behind, it will cost you time and money. As you become more successful as an investor, your available time is more valuable and not as available. If you get mired down in a bookkeeping problem, you will be robbing yourself of valuable time. And in the real estate investment world, time is big money. Tracking of all your business transactions must be kept current because the further behind you allow your books to become, the more likely you will forget how you spent that money.

When you set up your books for your business, make sure you have or get a credit card with rewards for using it. Here are a few of the reward cards that I like: Southwest Airlines (For 50,000 free rewards points out of the gate, go here: https://www.referyourchasecard.com/226/52Q1V3M02G). Presently, because of all the expenditures for my rentals and flips that I assign to the card, my Southwest rewards allow me and my immediate family to fly for free. Let me phrase it another way: I do not pay for anyone in my family to fly; the credit card company does. [Remember my rule about "Who is paying for this? Same idea.] Capital One also has a very good rewards program. My next card will be the Apple Card, which has a cash-back benefit. The essential thing is for you to get a card that "rewards" you with a benefit for spending money on real estate improvements. It takes money to make money, and you have to track the money you spend. If your actions, through the conduit of money, produce rewards, why not let the credit card company pay for the rehab and the trip to Mexico?

Bookkeeping is key to successful money management, but incorporating intelligent usage of your credit cards along with the accounting principle of stretching your term is also important. I pay all my credit card bills before they are due, so I don't pay any credit card interest. Try to do the same thing - paying interest on a credit card is not smart if you can avoid it. The credit card companies get 2-4% from each of my merchants on every transaction. They spiff me with some travel and let me finance purchases for 24-30 days interest-free, so everybody's happy. If you want to get creative, you can also use balance transfers from one card to another to lower or eliminate interest.

Have as much fun as you can with bookkeeping, but just be sure you are using the proper accounts for the proper books. Good bookkeeping is based on solid principles, and you should learn to understand them. After all, it's your money that is being kept. Get opinions from smart people about methods and people they use for their books. Not all bookkeepers are aces. I have had a few that were just data entry, with no knowledge of full accounting. I learned that a good bookkeeper has a basic understanding of the principles of accounting. Bookkeeping and accounting have a symbiotic relationship. If you have a good accountant, they should be able to keep you out of audits and guide you through the sometimes choppy waters of taxes; but the accountant relies on your books - if your books are wrong, then GIGO (garbage in, garbage out). If you get audited, your books and your accountant will matter big time. The taxman only cares about what you can show, prove and draw the line to. Don't rely on your memory!

OK, I know it's bookkeeping, so what's the big deal? Yes, there's an app for bookkeeping, too. So if you're doing your own books because you're small, write "Travel For Work To Buy Property" on your hotel receipt, so that you can deduct it. Then snap a picture of the receipt within your app and load it in. It's never been easier to keep track of the digital footprint you leave everywhere. I never want another audit. I am very thankful it happened early on when I was poor, young, and didn't have any bad habits. I just had a bad accountant. That lesson taught me this: books and accounting go hand in hand.

If you're a small-time investor, you can set up notifications with your credit card company, so the minute that your money is spent, you can record it in your phone notes or wherever you find convenient. There are multiple ways to keep track of things, but if you don't know how much money you lost or made, your returns (profits) are really going to go down because you won't be able to claim deductions on your taxes. If you spend cash, keep track of that too. Keep track of everything. Make sure the bookkeeping is done continually and is audit-proof.

Part of what I learned in my first audit back in 2008 was that even though the forms my accountant sent to the IRS looked proper, the bookkeeping didn't match. Good bookkeeping is your backup plan; if the IRS audits you, they will find a clear trail of how your accountant arrived at the numbers.

Top tip: Your books should back up what your accountant files on your taxes, so your accountant and your bookkeeper need to function together. I suggest that those tasks be performed by two separate people so they can check on each other. If you have one person doing both things and they make a mistake, they could potentially try to cover it up, so having two different people creates a system of checks and balances.

One thing I've always done is have my bookkeepers code things to how I think, which is memos and property lines. When I write a check or send an ACH (Automated Clearing House), which is an electronic fund transfer made between banks and credit unions, I make a specific note to describe what the repair was. For example, if you write a check to replace a water heater at 123 Elm St, then write "123 Elm St, water heater" on the memo line. When you look back to try to determine why a certain check was written, instead of spending valuable time questioning why that amount was paid to whomever, it's a lot easier when it's right there on the memo line. This would seem like common sense, but over the years, I've noticed that many bookkeepers don't think in terms of anything other than invoice numbers. If you keep those memos, then bookkeeping will be much more streamlined.

"Bookkeeping is also important when you need to raise money with partners. They're going to want to see your books."

When prospective investor partners encounter a person who says, "It's a cash business, and that's how I do things," the partners are going to take a hard look at the investor and assume that they're not honest; that they must pocket their money and steal from the IRS. In real estate, if you want to partner with somebody with integrity, it's imperative that you disclose everything upfront. If you're looking to avoid paying taxes, you need to look for tax strategies, not cheat the IRS out of money. Not only will that create a problem for you down the road, but it will also show your potential partners and other people you encounter in the future that you're a dishonest person. Most importantly, you need to learn from your mistakes, and good bookkeeping will lay it out clearly for you in black and white. Finally, how can you clearly know what your profit or loss is if you're cooking the books? That mafia lame brain criminal stuff is short-sighted and will get you in more trouble than you want. Embrace the rewards and perks from spending your hard-earned money. If you play your cards just right, the cashback from your credit card could pay for the salary of your bookkeeper.

CHAPTER

SIXTEEN

WHAT IS THE 1031 EXCHANGE?

IT'S THE TAX Strategy that Will Save You TONS of Money. How does deferring your taxes forever sound? Sure, that sounds impossible, but even if you can't defer the taxes forever, section 1031 of the Internal Revenue Code could allow you to defer your capital gains taxes for a significant period of time. Even better, you are allowed legally to use untaxed gains to further your growth even more. The 1031 exchange is one of the pillars of the robust American economy, and it's one of the great reasons to become a real estate investor in the U.S.A. That being said, 1031s can get complicated, so you should have a tax advisor who is well-versed in the details of these exchanges.

Here's a summary of how a 1031 exchange works: If I purchase an investment property for $100,000, hold it for 5 years, then sell it for $160,000, the capital gain would be $60,000. I will then engage a qualified intermediary (QI), who will hold the proceeds of my sale while I'm looking for my exchange 'like-kind' property(ies) that are valued at least one dollar more than the sales price of the original property. In other words, to get a full tax deferral on my gain, I need to purchase a property with a value of at least $160,001. If I buy a property that's less expensive, then I'll only have to pay tax on the difference/gain. I am also allowed to buy a more expensive property if I want.

Depreciation recognizes the yearly wear and tear of a property and is the cornerstone for 1031 exchanges. On residential properties, allowable depreciation is the purchase price divided by 27.5 years. On commercial properties, it's 39 years. Let's say I buy a property in Las Vegas for $20,000 and five years later decide to sell it for $185,000 – obviously, there is going to be a gain, even after deductible renovations. If I sell for more than the depreciated value of the property, I'll have to pay back the taxes that I didn't pay over the years due to depreciation unless I do a 1031 exchange.

What used to confuse me about a 1031 exchange is I thought it was an all-or-nothing type of deal, meaning that if I didn't hit the exact number on the subsequent exchange purchase, I would have to pay the full penalty on the total amount of gain. That's not true – you only pay tax on the amount that is less than the full deferral.

There was a situation in Kansas City, Missouri, where I was buying several houses using a 1031 exchange after selling a number of properties in Las Vegas. One of the sales fell through, and we were unable to complete that deal. The 45-day time frame that the IRS allows me to identify the exchange property(ies) had already lapsed, so I didn't have any more time to identify another property to do a full 1031 exchange. Was that going to blow up my whole exchange, and would I have to pay taxes on the entire large gain? Was I going to lose $40,000? No. I had to pay the taxes on the lesser gain or the amount of money that could not be exchanged. That true-life example illustrates a fundamental and important part of a 1031 exchange that you need to understand to take full advantage of this tax strategy.

Here is where you can really do well with a 1031 exchange. If you're investing long term and you're looking to get more cash, you may want to consider refinancing a property to pull out equity money tax-free, and then do a 1031 exchange on the property. When you pull capital out of the property, you will have money in your pocket. On paper, you'll just be exchanging the gain into another property. It sounds more complicated than it really is; just be sure to do the proper 1031 paperwork when you sell a property in order to refrain from paying taxes. The whole point of the 1031 exchange is to keep investors investing, which keeps a whole lot of people building, remodeling, selling, buying, and paying taxes. So do your part as an investor, and keep on using the 1031 exchange over and over and over again. America will thank you.

Ugly houses nobody wants can be turned into beautiful homes that can be rented for passive income or flipped for a good return. I paid $12,500 in 2021 for this place.

CHAPTER
SEVENTEEN
What Is the BRRRR Method?

BUY, REHAB, RENT, Refinance, Repeat. This is a very good method for those who are looking to start out in real estate investing today. Essentially, you're doing a flip to yourself and taking the refinance cash/capital to invest in another property; instead of selling a property to gain capital (and having to pay taxes on that money).

BRRRR is a great method to start within any size market. The fundamentals of this method are now a popular topic in the media, but they are the same fundamentals utilized by Real Estate Investors for decades. Simply put, investing in real estate gives you the capability to use renters, rehabbing, and refinancing to get access to your initial cash outlay and possibly some equity to reinvest. The BRRRR method works in both low and high-priced markets. When you grasp the concept, it's easy to forecast and scale your growth because you have all the data representing purchase, rehab, sale, and profit.

When you're utilizing the BRRRR method, you're buying a property under market value, and doing repairs to make it worth more than what you paid. Then you're refinancing it, hoping to pull out your original investment and more for reinvestment. Then you're going to do that again (repeat). Meaning you're going to find another property that you buy under market value, then rehab, rent, and refinance.

What makes the BRRRR method the best is that you can recapture your original investment and then some, so you can continue to buy more properties. The most important part of this method is to make sure that after you do the refinance, the rehabbed property cash flows. Meaning you can easily rent it out long-term or Airbnb it. You always want to make sure it cash flows and does it well.

You need to assess what your risk is.

Making $100 or $200 or less than the mortgage is probably not worth the risk, but it depends on how much that payment is. If it's a $1,000 payment every month and you project that you're going to be collecting $1,200 monthly rent, then I would say that it might be worth doing for the long-term value. Here's what I am trying to drum into your head. If you experience a single month of vacancy, your cash flow will go down substantially, especially if you are only cash flowing $100-300 per month. It is really hard to make up for losses, particularly if you are fairly new to investing. My suggestion is to have at least a $500 profit per month "cushion" on each rental property. Profit, also known as the spread, is what is left after your total costs (mortgage, taxes, insurances, and other expenses) are subtracted from your projected rent ($1,500 rent minus $1,000 total costs equals $500 profit). Adopting my cushion policy will ensure that you are set up for success by allowing you to absorb the occasional vacant month without major consequences.

For example, if you're able to pull an extra $100,000 out of a property, in addition to your original investment, and manage to earn another $1000 a month by reinvesting that $100,000, then you have significantly added to your total return from the original investment. There are a lot of important factors to analyze, but in general, the better the property cash flows, the more it makes sense to refinance and reinvest. Ideally, you want a low loan, low debt, high cash flow, and the ability to pay off debt with rental income.

> **"The most important thing that I like about the BRRRR method is that it allows you to build up your capital on a quick, tax-free route."**

This means you're able to take the money out for reinvestment, but you don't get taxed on the proceeds from your refinanced property. You're able to focus on buying properties for cash flow while learning how to repair them, so you come to understand the whole strategy of investing.

That's why I like BRRRR. Think of it as a flip that you don't sell, meaning you are able to take the "profit" from refinancing it, but you get to keep the property. This method teaches through your own efforts that you have to find a valuable deal, locate tenants, calculate rents, mortgages, insurance, and also how to refinance. These are the most important things you need to know when you look at investing in successful real estate flips. Let's summarize what BRRRR teaches you:

- How to find a good deal that includes a decent mortgage and insurance
- How to deal with lenders for refinancing
- About construction/how to repair
- How to analyze the market for sale or rent
- How to deal with tenants

CHAPTER

EIGHTEEN

Buying Properties with A Clouded Title

WHAT IS A clouded title? It means that there are defects in the title, and you probably won't be able to get title insurance on the property. Because of that, a traditional financial lender is not going to loan you money on a property until the defects in the title are cured.

For me, as a buy-and-hold investor, I don't care. To clarify, if I can get a property for the right price, I don't really care about a clouded title. For example, a partner and I own a duplex property in Louisiana that we bought in a tax sale. We own 96% of the property. We can't close out the other 4% of the property, but we have a controlling share, so we can rent it out. Over ten years of ownership, we can cure the title, but we can't sell it to anybody with a loan until we have a clean title. We got into the deal with a $3,000 acquisition and some rehab, and it will cashflow $700 on one side and $800 on the other side every month. When you look at a clouded title in that way (that you don't have a problem owning a property without a pristine title), then it doesn't become an impediment to making a deal. Each clouded title deal has to be examined very carefully, of course, but the takeaway is to take a closer look before looking away because you may be able to get a great cash-flowing property.

In real estate investing, the reason you're buying real estate is to get positive cashflow. Do you have controllable interest in the property? Can you cure the defects in a long-term 10-year hold strategy? Can you hire an attorney to do a quiet title now and fix the title issues over the long term if you plan to sell it? If you don't plan to sell it, do you really care? Are you going to leave it to your children, and is it something that matters?

I think that the people who are unwilling to buy a property with a clouded title are the same people who need to buy a brand-new, blemish-free appliance every time. If we have a little dent in the appliance and it works perfectly fine, I'm okay with buying it. I'm also okay with owning a piece of real estate where the title's not perfect.

If you need more peace of mind, then you'll need to determine what the risk is. Is there an old note on the title? Did someone pass away, and the note was issued 20 years ago, but the bank never foreclosed on the property? Is there a chance the bank is going to do that? Yes, there could be a small chance of that happening. How much money does the property need to be renovated?

When you're buying properties with clouded titles, you're usually getting them for next to nothing, and they are usually far from perfect. How much money are you willing to put into the property? You don't want to put too much money into a property with a cloud on the title unless your state allows for you to be reimbursed for what you lay out. Louisiana allows it so that state provides a certain degree of security for the investor making an investment.

If I have to put $50,000 into a property, and I could potentially lose that, then I have to ask myself if it's worth the risk. If it's a million-dollar property, and I could recoup the investment in ten months of renting it out, then it would be worth the risk.

Clouds on title are big-time payoffs if you have the patience and time to deal with them. They can also more than increase your return on investment (ROI) because you're buying inexpensive properties that other people aren't willing to risk their money on.

> "Strength and growth come only through continuous effort and struggle."
>
> - *Napoleon Hill*

Another cloud on title is partial ownership. If you have partial ownership and you have to fight with the other owners, that fight can be costly. Be careful when you play with clouded titles, there's a reason why the lenders won't insure them, but sometimes it's not that big of a deal. Evaluate the deal, talk to a smart attorney, make sure you can cure the title down the road, so your money won't be stuck forever!

CHAPTER
NINETEEN

Why You Need to Get a Lawyer

GET A LAWYER, then get another one, and one more after that. Meet with smart attorneys who are involved in real estate and can help you do things legally to advance your interests. Don't get somebody who's just looking to take your money; find one who's willing to teach you about how you can advance your interests as a real estate investor.

> **"If you are a real estate investor and you're in it for the long haul, the chances of getting sued are great."**

Don't be scared. Get your insurance in order. If you have established your business entity(ies), you're going to need to make sure that you have liability insurance. For one thing, liability insurance will be needed on pretty much every property you're going to own. If you get sued, tender that lawsuit to the liability insurance. Know that it's just a part of the deal.

Chances of you getting sued increase with the more properties you own, just as the odds of you getting into a car accident and getting sued increase the more you drive. It's all about insurance and liability - having insurance to cover your liability versus your asset. Some attorneys get a bad reputation because they just look to sue people and make money. That's what they've chosen as their profession, even though we might not appreciate them doing their job when we are in the crosshairs. Then there are others who can really help you because they understand how they can be a good resource for you. For example, your attorney may be aware of a law that's going to help you on a property that you want to buy.

Let's say you have a contract for a property for $100,000, and you know the property is worth $200,000. You've already tendered your earnest money, and you're ready to close on the property. Then the deal goes sideways, and the seller tries to sell to another party for the same price. At that point in time, you're going to talk to the seller and try to get them to perform, but if they aren't willing, you need to seek an attorney's advice. Your attorney will advise you how best to compel the seller to honor the terms of the contractual agreement you had in place.

What's that advice going to cost you? Generally speaking, you're going to need to make sure to protect your interest, so that the property can't be sold to another party for the price you agreed to purchase. That doesn't mean you want to litigate and force the seller to sell; you just want to stop them from selling it to someone else. This is the cheaper way of handling that situation.

On the other hand, if you get involved in a lawsuit, it's going to cost you a bunch of money. Alternatively, you may want to tell the seller you're going to sue for specific performance and then draft a lawsuit to show them the legal complaint before filing it with the court. If they are reasonable, they probably will want to answer the complaint. In general, because everything is clearly put in front of them, they are going to be compelled to do the right thing; unless they have another reason (unknown to you) not to do so.

Always look to lawyers for good advice, but one lawyer can't be everything. There are people who specialize in different fields of law: Some do probate, some do real estate litigation, some do taxes, some do personal injury. In everything that you will encounter, you're going to have to deal with attorneys, and they're not anybody to fear. They're just people with a job to understand the law, and their understanding of the law is different from somebody else's understanding. You need to make sure you're always playing by the rules and that you're running stuff by attorneys when you feel like there is risk involved, because you want to make sure you get good advice from a smart attorney.

> "Winners are not afraid of losing. But losers are. Failure is part of the process of success. People who avoid failure also avoid success."
>
> - *Robert Kiyosaki*

****

CAUTIONARY TALES

I have worked hard to keep this book informative and upbeat. Deep down to my core, I am an optimist and always try to look at the glass as half full. Still, I believe it's my responsibility to give you a complete picture.

From the time we are born, everything we do comes with some sort of risk, whether it's eating breakfast at the local Mom & Pop's or diving into the community pool. That goes for investing in real estate. I told you at the beginning that you should use my book to learn from my successes, mistakes, and failures. The following stories are not meant to discourage you; they are to enlighten you so that you are prepared for what could happen before it does. From my viewpoint, you will gain knowledge without pain and therefore be in a position to have even more success than I have had.

Let me start by giving you some good advice: Limited Liability Companies (LLCs) are the method I use for anonymity, asset protection, and reducing taxes. A trust that owns your rentals will pass those assets to your family free of most burdensome taxes. Nonprofits are excellent legacy plays to donate your property, as well as control the property, but it's a good idea to have the nonprofit pay you to run the operations. There is a lot involved with LLCs, but the bottom line is this: Whatever you buy as an investor, make sure it's not in your personal name and that you have insurance for liability at the bare minimum. When you are starting your business, get a lawyer who has a thorough understanding of all corporate structures, especially LLCs.

I have been in several lawsuits for real estate-related matters, both as the plaintiff and as the defendant. I have never gone to trial, but I have been deposed several times and spent hundreds of thousands of dollars on attorneys. In my experienced but humble opinion, litigation is silly. Always try to work things out by being a voice of reason, even if the other party is not willing to do so. Abandon all your pride and continue to try to work it out. Attorneys get paid big bucks to mount or fight lawsuits, and there's usually no-win for anybody at the end of them after you add or subtract the money involved. Use the legal system to assert your rights if you have to and fight off meritless lawsuits. Remember, the LLC is on the hook in a lawsuit, and if the LLC dies, you live. The LLC also offers asset protection from creditors, making it hard to collect on judgments.

Lawsuits are something that just happens in business. If you have to go through one, learn from the experience and evaluate what you could have done better. I will give you a quick example. Four or five years ago, I was in the process of starting to flip in an area of Vegas called Hyde Park. One thing I often do is concentrate my efforts for a time in certain areas, because I get to know what's happening; I also am making the comps and get a paper view of the money action. If I go into an area and do well on my first flip there, I'll consider doing the next one. I started flipping in Hyde Park. One led to two, and next thing you know, I was buying everything I could get my hands on. During that time, I found a house that was boarded up and had been abandoned for years. I discovered that the person who had owned it passed away; the sister or some distant relative was the administrator of the estate. I was following up with her, and towards the end of the conversation, she told me she had started working with a real estate agent. I said to myself, "Really, when did that happen?" I had not seen the property on the market. She gave me the agent's number, and I called her. She confirmed that she was the listing agent, and indeed, she already had an offer from an investor. Turns out I knew the investor, and we agreed to partner. The agent took our offer, except we never received a signed contract. However, she opened the escrow, so we turned in the deposit. She let us know in writing that our offer was accepted, but the seller never signed or returned the agreement. It was really starting to smell like a three-day-old fish. Finally, all the lies that the agent was telling both the seller and me put us at odds. I told the agent that I was going to force the issue. The seller's nephew reached out to me, and I bought the house directly from the seller. Then I sued the agent for damages. Statutory damages for this were only $3,500.

The attorney I hired gave me that piece of news after I had already committed $45,000 in legal fees to her. I decided to learn my lesson: Stuff happens, and you cannot be the guy who fights every battle.

That event changed my entire view of the legal system, and I reached several conclusions: 1) Who cares if you are right, you have to pay to prove it. 2) I had them where I wanted them with the *lis pendens* (an official notice to the public that a lawsuit involving a claim on a property has been filed), which is what I filed on the property to protect my interests. Finally, use an attorney to make money, not find "lawsuit" money. You are not in control of that outcome; it is a very long, expensive journey filled with steps set in place by law to pay attorneys to follow a case calendar along with all the other legalese. It's really not a good use of your time.

If you want to avoid getting sued, have liability insurance for your business and make sure you check your ego. Remember, don't cave when someone threatens to sue you, but the earlier you settle, the better. Once some people start spending money on lawyers, they lose all sense of reality. I have heard about lawsuits bankrupting people and/or eating up years of their good time. I can speak about this because I am on a few of those journeys right now. My advice is if you get sued, accept it, don't be mad. Instead, reflect: What did you do incorrectly? Were you wrong? Try to settle, try to work things out with the person who is mad at you - you can always talk to them directly, unless of course, they won't talk to you. Keep in mind, they may not talk to you and may just say I am telling my attorney! It can get very juvenile. Just keep trying, jettison your ego, and keep fighting if you have to. Again, with good liability insurance, the insurance company attorneys will fight for you, and you will just show up when needed and tell the truth.

Re-read Chapter 19, Why You Need to Get a Lawyer (and stay out of trouble). Also, don't think it can't happen to you! I know some people who have never been in lawsuits, but I know others who can't seem to avoid them. As I look back, I think of all the time and money I used to prove something insignificant and say out loud, "That certainly was a waste of time and money; what did I learn? Not enough."

Here's a funny story. The first time I got sued was over a commercial laundry appliance set. I sold a pair of 4 plexes to an investor who made me a cash offer on the properties. I sold them for $140,000 each. I bought each of them for around $70,000 and had held them for 6 years. The market was good, and I was tired of the area that the property was in. The quality of tenants was never that great, and I was ready to move on, so I was pleased with the sale. The investor who bought them must have been brand new or fairly unsophisticated. About a year later, I got a phone call from an attorney representing this investor, now the owner. He told me that the owner and the laundry leasing company were fighting because of the 15-year lease. I told him I had a 30 day out clause in the original leasing contract. He said, "Whaaat?!" We all ended up in court-assigned arbitration, where the outcome was coming from a Judge (attorney) who would listen to all the evidence and make a decision. At the end of the day, the lawyer and the owner sued the laundry company; the laundry company then sued them back; then they sued me, all over a lease that could have been terminated after 30 days (because I never was going to sign a 15-year lease). It was revealed that the sales representative from the laundry company never disclosed that he had a copy of my signed lease. The lease should have been delivered through escrow per language in the lease. Anyway, the new owner and his attorney got awarded $500 and some change, plus their attorney's fees, which was around $13,000. The attorney was a real piece of work. He told me if I helped him, he'd keep me out of it, and proceeded to get $500 for his client and $13,000 for himself from me and the laundry company (that had to be collected). I was so pissed after that case over a washer and dryer. The plaintiff was mad because the laundry company's service was poor. The other laundry company was fighting for their lease and right to service laundry. Two stupid lawsuits and I got caught in the middle. Finally, the attorney called me and asked if I was going to pay. I said, "Well, NO." He said, "We have a judgment, and we can put it into collection." I said, "Go ahead, it will take forever. You should have never taken the case and acted like you were trying to work it out, and then do an about-face and sue me." He was awestruck, so that's when I hit him with, "I am willing to pay the judgment, but on my terms: $500 per month for ten months, take it or leave it." He knew that 90% of judgments are uncollectible because they are hard to enforce without a sale, and it would really cost him a lot of money to enforce $5,000, along with time and energy. I also had called him out about acting like a nice guy but then playing nasty. I learned a few lessons: Make sure anything that transfers with the property goes through escrow; people will sue for silly items; attorneys win and clients lose when that happens. Invest your money in a good legal strategy to work with good attorneys for real estate-related matters: Solving issues with title and other encumbrances and probate; avoiding litigation whenever possible.

The other crazy thing I learned was that the laundry company knew they had a lease; they knew that the new seller didn't have the latest copy. Nonetheless, they were willing to go to court to protect a lease that was invalid because the new seller "violated" the current terms. I have seen this company in other actions with Homeowners Associations (HOAs). They have an attorney on staff. For them, protecting their lease space is their business model. Instead, they should be trying to improve their customer service.

This wasn't a huge deal for me, and stuff happens. If someone chooses to be wronged, they have a legal course, but that's an expensive route for both involved parties. Work things out, use attorneys for business, hire attorneys for their expertise, and don't trust anyone. :)

CHAPTER

TWENTY

Why Negotiation is Important

WHY DOES IT help to know how to negotiate in real estate? Negotiation is the single fastest way to save money when buying properties. Becoming an expert negotiator is probably one of the best tools that I have acquired. I once heard the fastest way to make money is by negotiating well. Think about that: Whether it's actual cash or terms or anything else in a contract, when you're negotiating, money is usually on the table, to be made or lost.

I have a personal friend who was a client from my time working at a radio station. John Wurts, the founder of Super Supplements, is an excellent negotiator. He could always find the bottom line after going into a negotiation, without knowing upfront the lowest amount a seller would take. Good negotiators know what's important to the person they're dealing with. They know how to press and how to spend the right amount of money; they know how to turn screws the right way.

John was willing to spend enough money for radio ad time, but he wanted to make sure he had the right number of ads on the radio to get what he was paying for, and then he would continue to renegotiate after the fact. He would just keep going until he was explicitly asked to stop, and that's what made him such a strong negotiator.

"A good negotiator is someone who not only gets a good deal; he also makes everybody else excited about the fact that they're doing business with him."

Good negotiation is an art that's hard to explain, but you need to work on learning this art to get the best returns on your investments. My favorite author on the subject of negotiation is a guy named Roger Dawson. He has written books like "The Power Negotiator" and "The Secrets of Power Negotiation," among others. I highly recommend reading those two if you want to learn some valuable negotiating skills.

One negotiating tactic Dawson shares is that when someone gives you a price, you should flinch, because it's a nonverbal expression showing you are in shock that the price is so high. When you're starting to negotiate a price with the seller and they tell you the price is $1,000,000, and you respond as if it's no problem, that's not going to leave you any room to negotiate. Instead, if you repeat that number of $1,000,000 as if you're in shock, then you're going to emphasize that's too much money, and right away, the seller might think, "maybe I need to lower my price."

> **"There are a lot of different tools that you can use when negotiating. You always want to get something. If somebody asks you for something, then you need to ask something from them in return. This is the essence of good negotiation."**

That technique tends to stop the grind of negotiation. For example, if I ask you if I can spend the night at your house and you say, "Sure, you can spend the night at my house as long as you give me $100," then I'm probably not going to ask to spend the night at your house anymore. You have to give them your problem or ask them for something in return.

Early in my career, I had people constantly asking to borrow money from me. I'd tell them, "I would love to lend you the money, but I have to deal with an IRS issue first." We all have taxes to pay. People won't ask anymore after that. You turn down their borrowing request in a nice way, while you let them know that it's not their business to know exactly why. Give them your problem and never accept their problem. Give their problem right back to them. That's the secret of good negotiation; give their problem right back to them and see how they respond to it.

"It's always good to be underestimated."

- *Donald Trump*

WHAT'S NEXT?

THANKS FOR READING this book – it's my first one, so I hope you enjoyed it. Now, you should be ready to take action in real estate investing, whether you agree or disagree with my way of thinking and doing things. Every day, more millionaires are created through passive income than any other way by using its tremendous energy to pay off continual reinvestment in real estate.

Passive income can pay for your cars, kids' college, vacations, and retirement. It can send you into a realm of wealth that will cause you to look back and think, "How did that happen?" Money passes through our hands, and we have to park it somewhere, so it doesn't end up as a liability. People need a place to live – you can provide that home, you can be creative and subdivide the land and build things. You can do everything your heart desires, but only if you start. What I've written about has been done by many people for years, and you won't die if you start. You will start living.

Michael Zeller, CEO of Flying Truss LLC, has a plan to transform the Rock Island bridge in Kansas City into an event center. I think it's a great idea, and have invested in the project.

Unless you are one of the few Americans whose job has a huge effect on the rest of us, such as the President or the CEO of Amazon or some major company, then what do you have to lose? Remember, Steve Jobs got fired from Apple by the man Jobs brought on as CEO, John Scully. That was one of the best things to happen to him. Initially, it killed him emotionally because the new leader of Apple, the company he started in his garage with Steve Wozniak, fired him. Jobs went out with something to prove and started a bunch of companies. But Apple was his baby, and the chip on his shoulder eventually led him back there to invent the iPod and iPhone. Maybe, you've got a chip on your shoulder like Steve Jobs or me, and you've got something to prove. Or maybe your reason is one where you just want to take care of your family and help others. Maybe, you are trying to find yourself, be what you want to be, and you are not sure who that is. Real estate will help you find yourself. Your true style will start to develop. Even as a realtor, I never dealt with offer submissions or contracts; I hired Transaction Coordinators to do that for me because I need to focus on my strengths. Now, I love laying out houses and solving problems with real estate, turning an ugly home into a pretty one, fixing something that everyone thought could not be done. I like to be told; you can't do that! Then I do it. Whatever your reasoning is, it doesn't matter. Don't make others rich by investing in their companies, their stocks, their real estate. Invest in yourself, in your real estate, in your financial education. You will never look back if you take action. Remember, I failed in the beginning, and look how it turned out. I know others who started later than me and who blew past me, and I know others who started with me, blew past me, then made a bad decision, and now are rebuilding. Scarcity is a mindset, don't be afraid of what others are doing, just be afraid of not doing anything. There are going to be people who just do better than you for a while, but discipline over longevity will win out. I see people who start, then quit, then try this, then try that. Real estate investing is proven; you don't need to experiment.

Prove that it works for you, then you can take risks, such as investing in a bridge (check out my YouTube video interview with Michael Zeller, who is building a city on a railroad bridge: https://www.youtube.com/watch?v=mUCN1WSgZNk. However, that was not my first, second, third or fourth investment. When you invest in partnerships and joint ventures, you are not in control, so you have others to blame, but the decisions you make are yours, and you are the one who makes choices. Choices surround everything you do. I choose to take risks, and I choose to also mitigate risk with smart investments.

The first thing you need to do is go to www.troykearnschannel.com and register for our newsletter, which includes videos and free contracts to get you started on your journey. Also, go to Tik Tok, Instagram, Facebook and follow me there. Follow other experts, and then start your own journey on social media. For a FREE downloadable comprehensive glossary of real estate terminology compiled by the Federal Trade Commission (FTC), go to:

https://www.ftc.gov/sites/default/files/documents/one-stops/real-estate-competition/realestateglossary.pdf

The networking available through social media is my current journey, which was the reason for producing this book, so your support of my endeavor would mean the world to me. I post three videos per week on YouTube, and I try to provide you with value for free, presenting real-life houses that I fix all over the country. Show your support by liking the videos and commenting; we answer all your questions, and we might feature them in an upcoming video. Moreover, if you are interested in coaching, I will be providing mentorship coaching very soon on my website. I also have various courses on wholesaling, flipping, rentals, and commercial property. I hope that our journey finds us together at a seminar in Belize next to Robert Kiyosaki, enjoying the fruits of our labor while someone else pays for it.

There's a great big country out there waiting for you. Let's roll!

REAL ESTATE INVESTMENT RESOURCES

Now that you have a basic understanding of how you can get started investing in real estate, here are a few ways you can take the next step to make your dreams come true:

1. Watch my YouTube videos on the Troy Kearns Channel for educational and how-to videos, as well as inspiration and insight. https://www.youtube.com/c/TheTroyKearnsChannel

2. If you haven't done so already, sign up to receive free resources about events (including coaching, mentorship, and educational opportunities) from my website. www.troykearnschannel.com.

3. Follow me at Troy Kearns on TikTok, Instagram, Facebook and Twitter. Watch out for my next "Millionaire Mentorship Contest." If you're a newbie investor, you could win up to $20,000 to jumpstart your new career!

4. Download the DealMachine app to get started on wholesaling. It doesn't matter where you live; if you find a good deal, I'm interested! Use this link: https://dealmachine.app.link/troy

5. I never pay for flights for myself or my wife and kids. Would you like some free flights? Use my preferred rewards card from Southwest Airlines when you spend money. It's a great card! https://www.referyourchasecard.com/226/52Q1V3M02G

6. You're going to need forms when you do real estate transactions. We have many free forms for real estate investment at my website, www.troykearnschannel.com.

7. For a FREE glossary of real estate terms from the Federal Trade Commission (FTC), go to: https://www.ftc.gov/sites/default/files/documents/one-stops/real-estate-competition/realestateglossary.pdf

Finally, do your own research, but just GET STARTED!

ABOUT THE AUTHOR

From a very early age, I had a desire to make money, and I was willing to put in the work to earn it. I went from mowing lawns at eight years old to delivering newspapers at 11 and onto my first "real" job at Burger King at 15. A year later, I got a job at Red Robin, where I stayed until I was about 24, to pay my way through college. Although I graduated from Central Washington University with my degree in communications, I don't believe people must go to college to become successful unless a profession, such as engineering or law, requires a certain degree. In fact, if I were allowed to redo my life, college would probably not be a part of it. I would save four years of time and thousands of dollars that could be put into real estate investing.

With my beloved dog Napoleon at Zion.
RIP Nappy D.

During my senior year in college, I received an internship at Seattle radio station KQBZ. I turned the internship into a permanent position at the station as the Promotions Director. Shortly after that, I became a station Account Executive, aka salesman. Cutting my teeth in radio sales was paramount to laying the foundation for future success because I learned that I had true grit and could sell under pressure.

Client sales are based on relationships, and doing what you say you're going to do, or having a conversation about why you are not. One of the most important things I learned while making ad sales is that the amount of my commission check could be connected to decisions made by somebody who had no direct contact with my clients. This lesson taught me that if I wanted to make my own way, it was completely up to me. I had a desire to make money and had studied the stock market for much of my life. I invested and read lots of books by Warren Buffet, Peter Lynch and others, but the stock market just didn't excite me because I still felt like I was not in control of the outcome. Before I left for Las Vegas, I obtained my Real Estate license in Washington, and shortly afterward, Nevada. Selling more than 3,000 homes in a short span of time allowed me to become an expert negotiator and transactional realtor. The proactive moves I made eventually led me to real estate investing - only doing the work can teach you what words in a book or out of somebody's mouth cannot.

When I started investing in real estate, I really didn't know what I was doing, and it took years to learn my lessons by trial and error. I want to pass along my knowledge and experience to you, so you can avoid some of the mistakes I made and start living the life you've always dreamed about, through investing in real estate. One of my most influential mentors is Robert Kiyosaki, author of "Rich Dad, Poor Dad," which completely turned around my head. This is one of my favorite quotes from Robert, "In school, we learn that mistakes are bad, and we are punished for making them. Yet, if you look at the way humans are designed to learn, we learn by making mistakes. We learn to walk by falling down. If we never fell down, we would never walk."

Investing in real estate has taught me that when I do make a mistake, I learn how to do it right the next time by coming up with solutions to problems. If you are focusing on solutions, your mind is set right. A lot of people see the glass as half empty, but you need to learn to see it as half full. You're still going to make mistakes on the road to success, and that's not a bad thing. Just let me help you stay out of the major axle-breaking potholes.

I am not a professional financial planner or consultant; this book is simply my compiled advice to you as a real estate investor. My final piece of advice to you: Always get professional advice from qualified professionals.

Troy Kearns

REVIEWS

Troy Kearns fell out of the heavens for me 15 years ago. My life has since skyrocketed, by a quantum leap, to bliss... and that isn't overstating it! Troy's given me step-by-step directions to a life of financial freedom and happiness. Work is now optional because of Troy's keen business sense and passive income expertise. I've often said having Troy in my back pocket is like cheating because it's really not fair!

John S

Troy does exactly what he says; he brings it "Hot & Fresh." By that, I mean Troy has a true passion for what he does. Whether it's a business opportunity, a new income stream, an insight about an opportunity somewhere in the country, or a business with great ROI, he's going to share the information he's used successfully to conquer the idea he's considering. From my experience, that's all about finding creative ways to make money, mostly involving real property transactions. I have firsthand experience with Troy's passion for business, including his incredible and somewhat prophetic insights for capitalizing on markets for the highest possible return. Personally and professionally, I've never been scared when I'm with Troy, which I don't say about many people! Whether we are in a dark alley or in a high-dollar real estate transaction, I know he's a guy I want on my side! Whatever you're looking to gain in life: whether it's a real estate portfolio or a fabulous example of passion and drive to achieve ALL your goals, Troy would be my top choice for direction. I'm blessed enough to have known him before he was a major success story, and let me tell you: He's the REAL DEAL.

Crystal S

Troy Kearns is not only my husband, he has been my best teacher, and lovingly refers to me as his first (and Number 1) student. From the very early days of our courtship, he was coaching me in real estate investing. When we first met, I was heavily in debt and not producing much income. In one year's time, I learned so much from Troy and made the decision that I wanted to do what he was doing to produce passive income. I began taking his direction and was able to purchase my first investment property, which turned into a flip. Since then, it's been a continuing "learn and earn" education from a consummate professional. Troy is out there making things happen constantly; he's in the real estate trenches day in and day out and then teaches in his "off" hours. Troy practices what he teaches and is passionate about what he does... In our household, we live and breathe all things REAL ESTATE…If you want what he has, then do what he does -- take the leap to learn from the expert!

Eden Kearns

Made in United States
Cleveland, OH
18 October 2026

46341970R00094